IDEAS & Issues

Pre-Intermediate

Geraldine Sweeney

Chancerel

Ideas and Issues Pre-intermediate

Editors	Carol Goodwright Liz Stock
Teacher's Guide Editor	Alison Burch
Designer	Gregor Arthur
Picture Researcher	Veena Holkar
Art work	Val Hill
Additional materials	Martin Hunt

ISBN	Student's Book	1 899 888 41 1
	Teacher's Guide	1 899 888 43 8
	Class Cassette 1	1 899 888 42 X
	Reading Cassette 2	1 899 888 56 X

PN 6 5 4 3 2 1 / 04 03 02 01 00 99

Published by
Chancerel International Publishers Ltd
120 Long Acre
London WC2E 9PA
England

Printed in Italy

The publishers and author would like to thank the following for permission to reproduce images:
Cover: Bubbles Photo Library, Jan Chipps Photography

Allsport/Mark Thompson p38, Eliot Schechter p39, p40, p41TR; Art Directors &Trip Photo Library p24M, p33; John Birdsall Photography p56BL, p64BL; BT Corporate Picture Library; a BT Photograph p42M, p42B, p43, p44, p45, p65; Bubbles Photo Library p10TR, p13, p45B, p48R, p54B, p55, p61, p62BM, p66, p68T, p69; Chancerel p20TR, BR, p49; Jan Chipps Photography p6TL, TM, TR, BL, BR, p8, p10BR, p16, p17, p23, p41BL, p42T, p48L, p56BR, p62TL, ML, BL, BR, p64TM, TR, BM, BR, p67, p68B; Colorific!/Mario Ruiz p52; Greg Evans International p9, p21, p35, p64TL; Mary Evans Picture Library p34, p50, p51; Fortean Picture Library p58, p60; Veena Holkar p12, p26T; Chloé/Mary McCartney p18; Rex Features p27, p54TR; RSPCA p22TR, BL; J. Sainsbury p26M; Dave Simson p6BM, p31, p32; Tony Stone Images p14, p24MR, p28M, p47; Telegraph Colour Library p7, p19, p24TM, BR, p37, p53, p56TL, BM, p59, p65; John Walmsley Photo Library p28T, p46, p56TM, TR, p62TR

Every effort has been made to trace the copyright holders of material in this book. The publishers apologise for any omissions and will be pleased to make the necessary arrangements when *Ideas and Issues Pre-Intermediate* is reprinted.

IDEAS & ISSUES

Pre-Intermediate

Contents

Contents

Focus

1 Before you read. It is important to teenagers to look fashionable or 'cool'. Write down two things that teenagers in your country wear and do to be cool. If possible, compare your list with a student from another country.

Read about it

2 Read what these British teenagers have to say about how to be cool in Britain.

"If you want to look cool, wear T-shirts with American cartoon characters like The Simpsons. *They are really 'in' at the moment."*

"If you really want to be trendy, have your ears, eyebrows or chin pierced, like me!"

"If you're into music, remember girl bands, like All Saints *are 'in' and boy bands like* Boyzone *are 'out'."*

"Don't try to push in at the front of a queue, if you want to be cool. British people hate it!"

"Remember to say "Wicked!", if you want to be trendy. People who are 'uncool' are 'sad'."

"If you like the latest thing, have your hands hennaed like me!"

trendy another word for cool
in *(in this context)* in fashion
out *(in this context)* out of fashion
a queue a line of people who are waiting for something
to push in to avoid waiting by joining a queue at the front

Hanging out with friends

3 **Find the answers to these questions in the texts.**

a How many words can you find that mean 'fashionable'?
For example: cool

b Are boy bands 'in' or 'out'?

c What don't you do when you join a queue of people?

d What are the coolest things to wear right now?

e What can you do to your eyebrows, if you want to be cool?

Key language

Look at these sentences.

If you like listening to music, remember girl bands are 'in'.

if + simple present, + simple present

Don't try to push in at the front of a queue, if you want to be cool.

simple present, *if* + subject + simple present

These are examples of zero conditional sentences. We use them for talking about rules and for giving advice. Notice that the present simple tense is used in both parts. The *if* clause can be at the beginning or the end of the sentence.

Now turn to page 72 for practice!

Talk about it

4 **What do you do to be cool? What do you think is uncool? Make lists. Use the topics below to help you.**

hair places to go things to do
clothes jewellery music

Now talk to another student.
Begin like this:

A What clothes do you wear if you want to be cool?
B Well, I wear ...
A What about music?
B If I want to listen to some really cool music, I ...
What about you?

Write about it

5 **Write a 'cool guide' for teenage visitors to your country. Tell them what to do and what not to do.**
Begin like this:

If you want to be cool in ... , then ...
Don't ...
It's cool to ...
It isn't cool to ...

It's hard to know what to say when you meet someone new.

Tune in

1 **Before you listen. Write down five questions you often ask when you meet someone for the first time. Compare your list with a partner.**

2 **Listen to Donna, Tim and Ellie talking about making friends. Listen and put a tick (✓) by any questions that you hear which are also on your list.**

3 **Listen to the dialogue again and answer these questions.**

a Does Donna find it easy to make new friends?
b What does Donna do at the youth club?
c Does Tim find it easy to talk to new people?
d What happens when Tim tries to talk to new people?
e What does Ellie do at parties?
f What does Ellie say to start a conversation?

Key language

Look at these questions you can ask when you meet someone for the first time.

- **Asking someone's name**
  What's your name?
- **Asking about age**
  How old are you?
- **Asking about school**
  Which school do you go to?
- **Asking about family**
  Have you got any brothers or sisters?
- **Asking about country/town of origin**
  Where are you from?
- **Asking about tastes in music/sport**
  What kind of music/sport *do you like?*
- **Talking about clothes**
  I like your jeans. *Where do you buy your clothes?*
- **Asking about friends**
  Do you make friends easily?

Now turn to page 72 for practice!

Sounds like this!

4 **Listen and repeat these questions from the *Key language*. Try to copy the speaker's stress and intonation.**

What's your name?
Where are you from?
How old are you?
What about you?
What kind of music do you like?
Do you make friends easily?
Have you got any brothers or sisters?

In questions that begin *'Wh'* or *How*, the intonation generally goes down at the end of the question. In questions which have a *'yes'* or *'no'* answer, the intonation generally goes up.

Talk about it

5 **Work in groups of four. Choose one person in your group to interview. The other three students must ask him/her questions. Listen carefully, you must not ask the same question twice! Then work in pairs. Take turns to interview each other.**

Working in groups is fun - but be sure to talk in English!

Write about it

6 **Write a description of the person you interviewed. Do not write the person's name.**
Begin like this:

He/she is from ...
He/she is ... years old.
He/she has got .../hasn't got any ...
He/she likes ... and ...

7 **Now read your description to your class. They must guess who it is!**

Focus

1 Before you read. Make a list of traditional roles for men and women.
For example, Women: mother, nurse
Men: father, bus driver
Do men and women still do the same type of jobs today?

A girl gang

Read about it

Girls are quiet, caring and home-loving, while boys are active, noisy and ambitious. This was the traditional view up to fifty years ago. But women's roles have changed since then. Girl Power is all around. Pop stars like Madonna and *All Saints* are teaching girls to be assertive and strong. There are women politicians, doctors and lawyers, women writers and artists. Young women are more confident than ever before.

It's great for the girls! But what's happening to boys? Now that women are earning their own money, men's traditional role of provider is disappearing: some women are choosing to bring up their children on their own and feel they don't need a man. Statistics show that boys are not doing as well at school as girls and are more likely to underachieve.

As a result, more young men are leaving school with few educational qualifications. This means poor job prospects. Young, single, unemployed men are more likely to become addicted to drugs and alcohol, get a criminal record and have car accidents than young women.

Let's hear what two teenagers have to say about Girl Power.

Naomi

"Girl Power says there are positive things about being female! Women want the same things as men - good jobs and money to spend. But we don't want to be the same as boys - boys are always trying to look cool in front of their friends. They don't share their problems and they don't talk about their feelings. Girls want boys to be more like them: open, sensitive and caring."

Ben

"I think Girl Power is rubbish! It's just making girls more like boys. Girls nowadays are going out in big groups. They are noisy and act just like lads. I think they look terrible - I don't want girls turning into *ladettes*!"

caring good at looking after other people
active lively, full of energy
traditional something that people have believed or done for a long time
Girl Power a popular idea that girls can do what they want
assertive good at saying what you want
to underachieve to do less well than is possible
a criminal record a police list of crimes a person has committed
ladettes *(slang)* girls who go around in big groups and act like boys or 'lads'

2 **Read the text again and answer these questions.**

a What is happening to traditional male and female roles?
b Why are some women choosing to bring up their children alone?
c Are boys doing as well as girls at school?
d What problems are boys more likely to have than girls?
e What does Naomi say about boys?
f Why doesn't Ben like Girl Power?

Key language

Look at these sentences.

Pop stars are teaching girls to be assertive.
subject + *be* + main verb + '*ing*' + object
Boys are not doing as well at school.
subject + *be* + not (*n't*) + main verb + '*ing*' + object

These are examples of the present continuous. We use it to talk about things that are happening in the present, either at this precise moment, or in the present time period.

Compare
John is doing his homework. (now, at this moment)
Girls are acting more like boys. (in the present time period)

Now turn to page 73 for practice!

Talk about it

3 **Work in groups of four: two boys and two girls, if possible. Read each of the following statements and discuss whether it applies to boys, girls or both.**

- They are loud, active and ambitious.
- They like chatting on the phone to their friends.
- They like to look cool in front of their friends.
- They like going around in groups.
- They are getting more confident.
- Their roles are changing.
- They behave badly.

Write about it

4 **What do you like and dislike about the opposite sex? Make lists, then write about your opinions. Use the model on the right to help you.**

There are ... things I don't like about boys/girls. Firstly, they ...

Secondly, boys/girls ...

However, there are several things I like about them. To begin with, they ...

Also, they ...

Tune in

1 Before you listen. Work in pairs and make a list in English of school subjects. For example: History, Maths

2 Listen to this interview with Tony, a Science teacher at a North London college and tick (✓) the subjects on your list that you hear.

3 Listen again and complete these sentences.

a The college has got .... students.
b They have evidence that .... do better in Maths and Science in single-sex schools.
c Boys have a lot more confidence doing ....
d Girls have a lot more .... than boys.
e Boys underachieve because ....
f Some mixed schools have ....

vocational subjects subjects that train you for specific types of job e.g. typing, metalwork
single-sex girls only or boys only
mixed classes classes with boys and girls
practical activities tasks you do with your hands
apparatus equipment
to compete (with) to be in competition
patience the ability to stay calm without becoming angry or agitated

Key language

Look at these sentences.

We have got about 3,000 *students in our school.*
subject + *have got* + object

Our school hasn't got a gym.
subject + *have/has* + not (*n't*) + *got* + object

Has your school got a swimming pool? *Yes, it has./No, it hasn't.*
have/has + subject + *got* + object?

We use *have* + *got* to talk about the things you can find in a school, town, house etc.

Now turn to page 73 for practice!

Sounds like this!

4 **Listen and repeat these questions. Try to copy the speaker's stress and intonation.**

Has your school got a swimming pool?
Have you got a gym at your school?
Has your school got a Science laboratory?

Science students at an English secondary school.

Talk about it

5 **Make a list of your school's facilities. For example; gym, Science laboratories, sports field**
Then, ask another student about his/her school.
Begin like this:

A Which school do you go to?
How many students has it got?
Has it got a ... ?
Have you got a ... in your school?
What subjects do you study?

6 **Look again at the list of school subjects you made in activity 1.**
Which subjects do you think boys or girls are better at? Why? Discuss your ideas with a partner.

Write about it

7 **Write a letter to your pen-friend in Canada. Describe your school and tell your pen-friend about the subjects you study. Use the letter on the right as a model.**

9, Elm Avenue
Brighton
East Sussex
BN6 5RG

20th July

Dear Tony,

Thank you very much for your letter. It was great to hear from you. You asked me about my school. Well, my school is a mixed/single-sex school. It has got about ... students. We have got ... My school has also got ... Unfortunately, my school hasn't got ... I study ...

Write soon and tell me about your school.

Best wishes,
Fiona

Shopping

Focus

1 Before you read. What do you like doing in your spare time? Make a list, then talk about it with a partner. Is shopping on either of your lists? If yes, why?

Read about it

The British love shopping and it has become a major pastime for many people. Do you love shopping? Are you a 'shopaholic'? Complete this questionnaire and find out! Put a tick (✓) in the box next to the best answer.

1 Do you go shopping at the weekend?
- ☐ **a** Always. I love shopping!
- ☐ **b** Sometimes. I don't mind shopping, but there are other things I want to do.
- ☐ **c** Never. I hate shopping.

2 Do you shop:
- ☐ **a** alone?
- ☐ **b** with friends?
- ☐ **c** with a member of your family?

3 How much do you spend?
- ☐ **a** Too much! I never have enough money for all the things I want.
- ☐ **b** Quite a lot, but I always have money left for other things I want to do.
- ☐ **c** Very little, I don't always spend money when I go shopping.

4 If a friend invites you to the cinema on a Saturday afternoon, do you:
- ☐ **a** refuse, because you prefer to go shopping?
- ☐ **b** agree, but feel you might be missing out on a bargain at the shops?
- ☐ **c** agree, you are often free on a Saturday?

5 Read these statements. Which one do you agree with?
- ☐ **a** A weekend without shopping is no fun!
- ☐ **b** Shopping is OK, but I enjoy doing lots of other things as well.
- ☐ **c** I don't enjoy shopping, I find it boring.

6 When the sales are on, what do you do?
- ☐ **a** I get there as early as I can, so as not to miss a bargain.
- ☐ **b** I sometimes go, just to have a look round.
- ☐ **c** I stay away from the shops at sale time. I hate shopping in crowds.

Now add up your points!

Score 3 points for every a) answer, 2 points for every b) answer and 1 point for every c) answer.

15–18: Oh dear! You really love shopping, and could be a 'shopaholic'. Try to develop some new interests which do not involve shops and spending money!

11–14: You enjoy shopping, but you enjoy other things too. You have a balanced attitude to shopping.

6–10: You hate shopping. Try visiting markets, they have a lot of character and are a good way to meet people. Shopping can be fun!

a pastime a hobby, a free-time activity

a shopaholic someone who loves shopping and cannot stop

to miss out (on something) to lose an opportunity

a bargain something for sale at a very good price

the sales a time when shops reduce their prices

to have a look round to look in a shop or place because you are curious

crowds lots of people in one place

Key language

Look at the faces and sentences below.

I love going to markets	*I enjoy going to markets*	*I don't mind going to markets*	*I don't like going to markets*	*I hate going to markets*

After verbs such as *love, like, enjoy, don't mind* and *hate* the verb which follows takes the *'ing'* form.
For example:
We don't mind going to markets.
Do you like visiting shopping malls?
She doesn't enjoy going to the sales.

Sometimes the spelling of the verb changes. If the last letter of the verb is: *p, r, t, r, m* or *l*, it is doubled before the *'ing'* is added. (There are exceptions, e.g. *waiting*.)

For example:
I hate swimming.
Sam enjoys travelling.

Now turn to page 74 for practice!

Talk about it

2 **Find out about your classmate's shopping habits! Look at this list of questions, write three more of your own, then interview a partner.**

- Do you like spending money?
- What do you like buying?
- Do you like hunting for bargains?
- What else do you like doing in your free time?
- ....
  ....
- ....
  ....
- ....
  ....

Write about it

3 **Write a paragraph about your partner's shopping habits. Use the questions you asked in *Talk about it* to help you. Use the example below as a model.**

My friend Roberto is Italian. He loves shopping with his friends on Saturday afternoons.

He likes buying designer clothes, when he has got enough money.

He enjoys ...

Tune in

1 **Before you listen. Make a list of different items of clothing. For example: T-shirt, jeans**
Then compare your list with a partner.

2 **Isobel and her friend Rehman are shopping. Listen to the dialogue and write down what they buy.**

REHMAN	This black one's nice.
ISOBEL	Hmm. Why don't you try it on?
REHMAN	Good idea. Excuse me. Can I try this T-shirt on, please?
ASSISTANT	Sure. The changing room's over there.
ISOBEL	What do you think?
REHMAN	It's a bit small. I'll ask if they have a larger size. *(To the assistant)* Excuse me. Do you have this T-shirt in a larger size?
ASSISTANT	Just a moment, I'll have a look. Here you are.
REHMAN	Yes, this one's much better. I think I'll take it.
ISOBEL	It looks nice. How much is it?
REHMAN	£12.99, reduced from £19.99. It's a bargain!
ASSISTANT	How do you want to pay?
REHMAN	Oh, I'll pay by credit card. *(To Isobel)* I won't pay for it in cash, I'll need some money later on.

to try (something) on to put clothes/shoes on to see if they are the right size
changing room a room in a shop where you can try clothes on
a bit a little
to have a look *(in this context)* to go and find out
reduced the price is lower than before
later on at a time in the future
cash money: coins and notes

3 **Listen again and answer these questions.**

a What colour is the T-shirt Rehman chooses?
b What is the problem with the T-shirt when he tries it on?
c Does the assistant find what Rehman wants?
d Does Rehman buy the T-shirt?
e How much does it cost?
f How does Rehman pay?

Key language

Look at these sentences from the dialogue.

I'll take it.
subject + *will* ('ll) + verb + object

I won't pay for it in cash.
subject + *will not* (*won't*) + verb + object

We use *will* future for decisions we make as we speak. For example:

Dave *The phone's ringing.*
Pete *OK, I'll answer it.*

Now turn to page 74 for practice!

Sounds like this!

4 **Listen and repeat these sentences from the dialogue. Try to copy the speaker's stress and intonation.**

I'll take it.
I won't pay for it in cash.
Can I try this on, please?
How much is it?
How do you want to pay?

Now work in groups of three and act out the dialogue in activity 2.

Write about it

5 Write a dialogue between a customer (Sonia), and a shop assistant. Sonia wants to buy a pair of jeans and asks the assistant to help her find the right size and colour.
Begin like this:

Sonia *Excuse me. I like these jeans, but have you got them in a larger size?*

Assistant *Just a moment, I'll have a look.*

6 When you have finished, act out your dialogue with a partner.

Be a designer!

Focus

1 Before you read. How many famous fashion houses can you think of? Make a list. For example: Valentino, Chanel

Read about it

2 The world of fashion is glamorous and exciting and lots of young people want to become fashion designers. Read this interview with young designer Stella McCartney of Chloé, Paris.

When did you decide you wanted a career in fashion?

When I was 15, I got a job with the fashion house, Christian Lacroix.
I enjoyed it so much I decided that fashion design was the career for me.

What did you do next?

I did my A levels and then took a year off before going to university.

Why did you do that?

I wanted to get some experience working in fashion. So, I stayed in London and I worked for the British designer, Betty Jackson. I also did some work for *Vogue*.

Where did you go to college?

I got a place at Central Saint Martin's College of Art and Design in London and studied for a degree in Fashion Design.

Did you find it difficult to get into college?

Oh yes! The college receives 600 applications each year for only 40 places! So the competition was very tough!

What did you do after you left college?

While I was at St Martin's, I noticed a lack of technical training, so I worked for a tailor in London's Savile Row for a while. Then in 1997, I got my present job with Chloé in Paris. They employed me as a fashion designer and I showed my first collection that year.

What kind of clothes do you design?

I like to think I design sophisticated clothes, combining masculine tailoring with traditional, feminine fabrics like satin, silk and lace. I like to add details, such as glass buttons and embroidery. I think my clothes are stylish, sexy and easy to wear!

3 Now answer these questions.

a When did Stella first decide on a career in fashion?
b What did she do between leaving school and starting college?
c Where did she go to college?
d When did Stella start her job at Chloé?
e When did she show her first collection?
f What kind of clothes does she design?

glamorous sophisticated, magical
A levels examinations English school students take at age 18
a degree the exam you take at the end of a university course
tough difficult, testing
role position, job
a lack (of something) a need
sophisticated elegant and refined
embroidery decoration made by sewing

Key language

Look at these sentences.

I decided that a career in fashion was for me.
I stayed in London.
I worked for Betty Jackson.

These are examples of the simple past.
To make the simple past of regular verbs we add *'ed'* to the infinitive form.
For example: work - work*ed*
We use the simple past to talk about events in the past which are now finished.

Compare

She works for Chloé. (at the present time)
She worked for Christian Lacroix. (at a time in the past)

To make questions in the simple past, we use the past form of the auxiliary verb *do* - *did*.
For example: *Where did you go to college?*

'wh' + *did* + subject + verb infinitive + object?

Did you find it difficult?

did + subject + verb infinitive + object?

Now turn to page 75 for practice!

Sounds like this!

4 **The *'ed'* endings of regular verbs in the simple past can be pronounced in three different ways. Listen and repeat.**

/t/	/d/	/ɪd/
worked	*stayed*	*decided*

Now listen to these verbs. Write each in the correct column according to how the *'ed'* ending is pronounced.

A Paris fashion show

Talk about it

5 **Work in pairs. One person is a reporter from the newspaper, *The Daily Tribune* and the other is the famous fashion designer, Sam La Crosse. Read your role card and prepare your part.**

REPORTER

Prepare to interview Sam La Crosse.
Write down the questions you would like to ask him.

SAM LA CROSSE

Prepare to be interviewed by a journalist.
Make some notes about your career in fashion design: how you got started, your career so far and what you are doing now.

When you are ready, begin like this:

Reporter Well, Sam, it's great to meet you.
First of all, wh ...?

Tune in

1 **Before you listen. Are you interested in fashion? Would you like to be a fashion designer? Why? Why not? Discuss with a partner.**

2 **Listen to this interview with Barrington Brown, who is studying men's fashion. What are his ambitions?**

3 **Listen to the interview again and answer these questions.**

a Where did Barrington go to school?
b What did he do in his spare time?
c What did Barrington do when he left school?
d Where does he get his ideas?
e What does he want to do when he leaves college?
f What does he say about menswear compared to women's fashion?

weird strange, unexpected
textiles cloth, fabrics
spare time free time
menswear men's clothing, particularly suits
veins *(in this context)* the pattern on a leaf
structure shape, form
outrageous bizarre, unconventional
to put (something) on the map to make something important, to bring people's attention to something

The coat Barrington designed.

Key language

Many English verbs are irregular. Here are the irregular simple past verbs you heard in the interview with Barrington.

infinitive	simple past	infinitive	simple past
be	*was/were*	*make*	*made*
go	*went*	*spend*	*spent*
get	*got*	*see*	*saw*
choose	*chose*	*put*	*put*
become	*became*		

Now turn to page 75 for practice!

Punks in London

Talk about it

4 **Work in groups of four and share your opinions on the questions below.**

Do you think that:

- young people spend too much time worrying about fashion?
- designer clothes are better quality than other clothes?
- it is silly to wear something just because it's the fashion?
- it doesn't matter what you wear, it is personality that counts?
- young girls should try to look like fashion models?
- boys don't care how they look?

Write about it

5 **Imagine that you would like to go to college to study men's fashion, like Barrington Brown.**
Write a letter to the college. Give details about yourself, why you are interested in fashion, what you would like to design and your ambitions.
Use this letter as a model:

7, Goldstone Rd
Brighton
East Sussex
BN7 3RJ
23rd April

The Principal
Northbrook College
Worthing
Sussex

Dear Sir or Madam,

I am ... years old and I am studying at ... I am very interested in ... and would like to apply for a place at your college.

I would like to design ...

My ambitions are ...

I look forward to hearing from you.

Yours faithfully,

Focus

1 **Before you read. Have you got a family pet? If yes, tell another student about it. Then, make a list of pets that people keep in your country.**

Read about it

A nation of animal lovers?

The British like to think of themselves as a nation of animal lovers. Sadly, this isn't always true - in 1997 alone, the RSPCA (Royal Society for the Prevention of Cruelty to Animals) investigated over 117,300 cases of cruelty. The charity rescues badly-treated animals, looks after them and tries to find them good homes. The RSPCA say that a lot of cruelty could be avoided, if people understood their pets' needs and the commitment involved in keeping an animal. Here are two case studies of animals they have rescued.

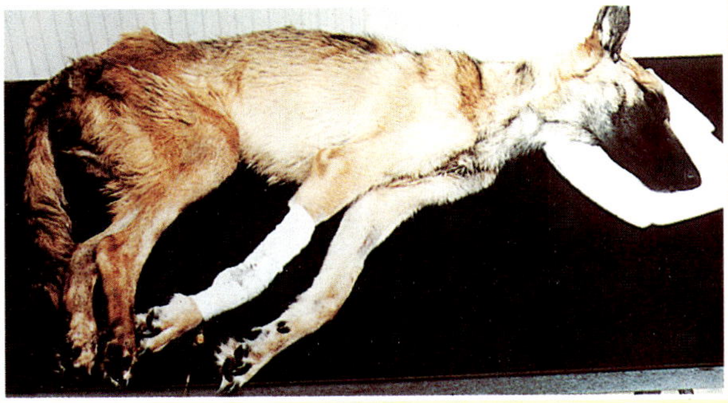

Billy

Billy's owner put him in a plastic bag and threw him out with the rubbish. Luckily, an RSPCA inspector found him. He was starving and so weak that he couldn't even lift his head. The RSPCA took him immediately to a vet, but he didn't expect him to live. Very slowly, Billy began to recover. Now he's in a new home and can enjoy life again.

Faith

An RSPCA inspector found Faith in a muddy field. She was in a terrible condition, and she was extremely thin. Happily, we weren't too late to save Faith. She now has a new home and is slowly putting on weight. Faith's owner, a horse dealer, was fined £250 and banned from keeping animals for life.

2 **Look at the text and find the answers to these questions as quickly as you can.**

a How many cases of cruelty did the RSPCA investigate in 1997?
b What did Billy's owner do to him?
c How much was Faith's owner fined?
d Where is Faith now?
e How do the British think of themselves?
f The RSPCA say a lot of cruelty could be avoided. How?

cruelty behaviour that makes an animal or person suffer

commitment hard work, effort needed to do something well

starving very close to death because of a lack of food

thin having no fat on one's body

to put on weight to increase the weight of one's body

a horse dealer someone who buys and sells horses

to fine to punish someone by making them pay a sum of money

Key language

Look at these sentences.

Dogs must have a lot of exercise.
You mustn't leave animals alone when you go on holiday.
subject + *must (n't)* + infinitive without *to* + object

We use *must* to talk about something which is essential or an obligation.
It is a modal verb and does not have the third person 's'
in its simple present form.
For example: *A dog must have a collar*.

Look at these sentences.
Hamsters need to live alone.
subject + *need* + infinitive with *to* + object

Cats don't need a lot of company.
subject + *don't/doesn't* + *need* + object

Need can also be followed by a noun.
For example: *Dogs need a bed to sleep in*.

We use *need* to talk about things which are necessary. *Need* here is an ordinary verb: it has the third person 's' in its simple present form:
A dog needs a garden to play in.

Now turn to page 76 for practice!

Don't buy a pet just because it's cute!

Talk about it

3 **Work in pairs. Think of a pet and write down three sentences about things the pet needs or must have to be happy and healthy. Read out each of the sentences without saying which animal it is. The other person must guess which pet it is.**
Begin like this:

A It needs .../You mustn't .../It must have ...
B Is it a ... ?
A Yes, it is!/No, it isn't. It's a ...
Your turn!

4 **Work in groups of three or four and discuss the questions below.**

- Why are people cruel to animals?
- Is there an equivalent of the RSPCA in your country?
- Do you think your country does enough to protect animals?

Tune in

1 **Before you listen. Look at the photos and match them with the correct name from the list below.**

snake iguana tarantula
Vietnamese pot-bellied pig

2 **You are going to listen to a radio programme called *Pet Phone-in*. As you listen, look at the photos and tick (✓) the animals which are mentioned in the programme.**

3 **Listen again and complete these sentences.**

a Sophie de Groot works at ....
b Nicky wants a .... because ....
c Nicky is going to keep his pet in the ....
d Rosie wants a ....
e Iguanas can grow up to .... long.
f People buy exotic pets because .... but often they don't ....

.... ☐

.... ☐

.... ☐

.... ☐

Key language

Look at the adjectives below and check any you do not know in the *Word list*.

fashionable	*playful*	*scary*
nervous	*gentle*	*slimy*
dangerous	*noisy*	*fun*
friendly	*quiet*	*ugly*
cuddly	*loyal*	*cute*

Adjectives can be placed before a noun: *A dangerous spider*, or after verbs such as *be*, *seem* or *look*: *Kittens are very playful. Tarantulas seem dangerous, but they are not. That puppy looks cute.*

Now turn to page 76 for practice!

a pet an animal which is kept in the home
a phone-in a radio or TV show where you can telephone and participate in the programme
an animal rescue centre a place where people can take lost, abandoned or cruelly-treated animals
an exotic pet an unusual pet, usually from a tropical climate
to look after *(in this context)* to provide an animal with all its needs
mice the plural of mouse
a vivarium a place to keep reptiles and insects

Sounds like this!

4 **Listen to the adjectives from the *Key language*. Place each in the correct column below, according to the number of syllables in each word, as in the examples.**

•	●•	●••
cute	*timid*	*dangerous*

Talk about it

5 **Work in groups of three or four. Look at the situations below and decide on a suitable pet for each household.**

- A young, working couple with two small children.
- A university student who lives with a friend.
- An elderly man who lives alone and cannot walk very far.
- A middle-aged couple with three teenage children.

Begin like this:

A I think a ... is a good pet for ..., because ...

B Yes, or how about a ...? They need/don't need ...

6 **Work in pairs and discuss the questions below.**

- Do you think people should be allowed to keep exotic pets, such as lizards and snakes?
- How can pet shops help people choose the right pet?

Write about it

7 **Choose an animal and write an acrostic poem about it. This is a poem where the first letters of each line spell a word, as in the example below.**

Food or poison?

Focus

1 Before you read. What is your favourite food? Ask three other students.

Read about it

Genetically modified soya

Scientists can now modify the food we eat to make it grow, taste and even look, better! The common soya bean was one of the first foods to be genetically modified. Many people though, are not happy with this new food. Our food expert answers your questions.

Q: What are soya beans?

A: Soya beans contain protein and fat. They are very common in foods such as margarine, bread, sweets and biscuits. Now, scientists can genetically modify, or change them.

Q: Why do scientists want to change them?

A: So they can make them grow bigger and stronger, even in poor soil. This means that farmers can grow more soya than they could before.

Q: How do they genetically modify a soya bean?

A: All living things have genes. In humans, genes decide your characteristics - for example, whether you have blue or green eyes. If you put a new gene into a soya bean, you can change its characteristics and make it better. Scientists do this by using bacteria and viruses to 'import' the new genes into the soya bean to improve it.

Q: Could there be problems with genetically modified food?

A: Yes. Because bacteria and viruses are used to modify food, scientists might create new diseases by mistake. We may not be able to cure these diseases.

Q: Why do we need genetically modified food?

A: Genetically modified plants will grow better and stronger. There will be more food and it will be cheaper, too.

Q: Not everyone wants genetically modified food. Will people be able to choose?

A: Food labelling will become a very important issue, if people are to have a choice. Not all food producers are in favour of this.

Soya beans

INGREDIENTS

VEGETABLE OIL, MAIZE, RICE FLOUR, ◆ DEFATTED SOYA GRITS, RUSK, SALT, DEXTROSE, YEAST POWDER, FLAVOUR ENHANCER: MONOSODIUM GLUTAMATE; FLAVOURINGS, YEAST EXTRACT POWDER, ONION POWDER, SPICE EXTRACTS, COLOURS: BETANIN, CAPSANTHIN.
◆ **PRODUCED FROM GENETICALLY MODIFIED SOYA BEANS.**

• CONTAINS SOYA, WHEAT & MILK

The label on a packet of.potato snacks.

to modify to change something's characteristics

soil the ground, where plants and crops grow

characteristics features

a virus a tiny organism which causes diseases

to create to make

to cure (a disease) to stop a disease and reverse its effects

to improve to make something better

2 Read the text again and answer the questions.

a What are soya beans?
b What kinds of food contain soya beans?
c What do genes do in humans?
d Are there any possible problems with genetically modified food?
e What are the advantages of genetically modified food?
f Why will food labelling become important?

Key language

Look at these sentences.

Possibilty

There will be more food.
Some people won't buy genetically modified food. — 100% (definite)

It could be the answer to the world's food problem. — 50% (fairly sure)
Scientists might create a new disease by mistake. — 20% (uncertain)

Will farmers grow more crops? *Yes, they will./No, they won't.*

We use *will*, *could* and *might* to talk about future possibilities. They are modal verbs, like *must* (see page 23). They only have one form and do not have the third person '*s*'.

Now turn to page 77 for practice!

Talk about it

3 What do you think will happen in the future? Talk about the topics below with a partner. Begin like this:

- work - in the office or at home?
- cars - petrol engines or electric engines?
- families - bigger or smaller?
- schools - better or worse?

A I think people will work at home in the future.
B Why?
A Because everyone will have a computer.

Will cars look like this in future?

4 Discuss these questions with your partner.

- Do you agree with the production of genetically modified food?
- Would you buy genetically modified foods?
- Is genetically modified food available in your country? Find out.

Write about it

5 Write an article for your school magazine about genetically modified soya beans. Begin like this:

Scientists can now genetically modify soya beans. This is worrying some scientists, but there are some advantages.
First of all, ... Also, ...
There are also some disadvantages. ...

Tune in

1 **Before you listen. There are many sayings about how foods affect us. For example: carrots are good for your eyes. Water is good for your skin.**
Work with a partner. Can you add to this list?
Are there any foods you can't eat, because they make you ill?

Paul

2 **Paul seems perfectly healthy, but like a growing number of people today, he has a dangerous food allergy. Listen and tick (✓) the foods listed below that Paul cannot eat.**

a peanuts	☐	e margarine	☐
b fish and chips	☐	f peanut butter	☐
c ice-cream	☐	g cheese	☐
d eggs	☐	h flour	☐

3 **Listen again and decide whether the sentences below are true or false. Then, correct the false statements.**

a Paul cannot eat peanuts.
b Paul's mother has to read the labels on the food she buys.
c Margarine sometimes contains peanut oil.
d Doctors think Paul's allergy is caused by a protein in the peanut.
e Paul has to carry adrenalin with him at all times.
f If he is ill at school, Paul's teachers can't help him.

peanut a type of nut which is often eaten salted, as a snack

tongue the soft, movable organ inside your mouth

pain the feeling you have if part of your body is injured

an allergy a reaction to something your body does not like

to be allergic to (something) to suffer an unpleasant reaction to something

to swell up to get bigger due to injury or allergy

an injection when a special needle is used to introduce a drug into the body

Key language

Paul often refuses invitations to eat out because he must know exactly what is in the food he eats. Here are ways of inviting, making suggestions, accepting and refusing an invitation.

- **Inviting someone**
  Would you like to go to the Indian restaurant?
- **Making a suggestion**
  Let's go to a pizzeria!
  Why don't we go to the snack bar?
- **Refusing an invitation or a suggestion**
  No, thanks. I'm not keen on pizza.
  No, thanks. I don't like the food there.
  No, thanks. I'm allergic to spicy food.
- **Suggesting an alternative**
  Why don't we go to the Chinese restaurant, *instead*?
  How about going to the new vegetarian restaurant?
- **Accepting a suggestion or an invitation**
  That's a great idea!
  Yes, let's do that!

Now turn to page 77 for practice!

Sounds like this!

4 **Listen and repeat these sentences from the *Key language*. Try to copy the speaker's stress and intonation.**

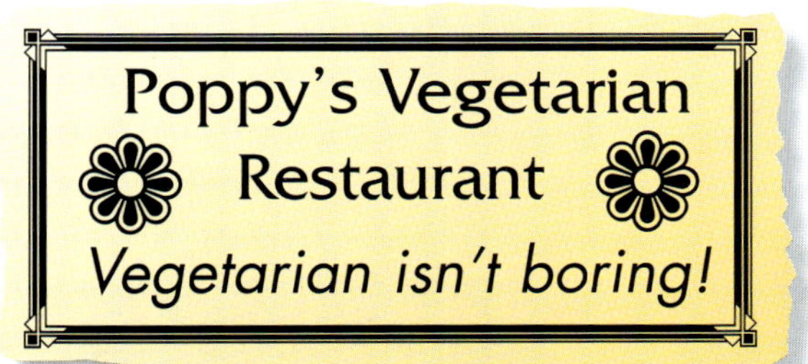

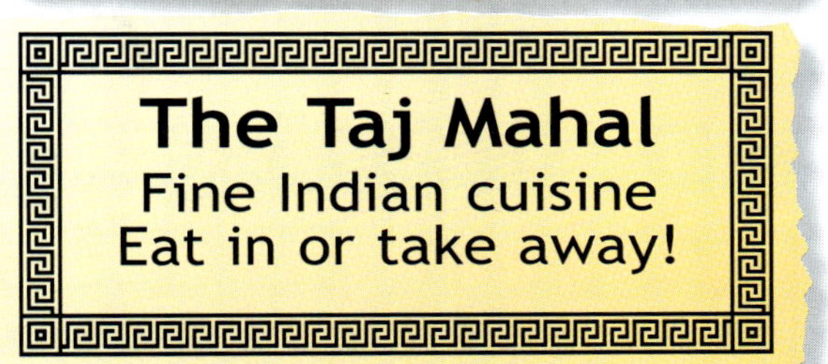

Talk about it

5 **Look at the four advertisements and decide where you would like to have dinner.**
Now work in groups of three and decide together where you are going to eat. Begin like this:

A Let's go to *Sergio's Pizza Place*. It looks good!
B No, thanks. I'm not keen on Italian food. How about going to the ...?
C Well, I'd like to go to ...

6 **Discuss these questions with a partner.**

- Does anyone you know have a food allergy? What foods are they allergic to?
- What can food manufacturers do to help people with food allergies in your country?

Focus

1 **Before you read. Do you ever go to restaurants? Who do you go with and what kind of food do you like to eat?**

Read about it

Rain forest in the heart of London!

If you can't afford to visit a real rain forest, you can experience one right in the centre of London! The *Rainforest Cafe* in Shaftesbury Avenue, is a unique restaurant and shopping adventure. You can eat there in the shade of tall trees, while you watch for animals hiding in the branches. All the animals you see are in danger of dying out. You'll hear the animals as well as see them. There is even a tropical 'climate' with thunder-storms every half hour!

to afford to have enough money to do something
rain forest jungle
dying out disappearing

Rainforest Cafe

A WILD PLACE TO SHOP AND EAT®

THE ADVENTURE BEGINS

salads

VOLCANIC COBB SALAD £8.95
Artfully arranged volcano style! Crisp greens, tender marinated chicken breast, blue cheese, black olives, tomatoes, chopped egg and bacon. Tossed with Paradise Balsamic Vinaigrette Dressing. "Feel the earth shake!"

THE AFRICAN WIND £8.95
Tender fried chicken tenders, piled high on top of fresh shredded lettuce, carrots, cheese and crispy fried onions. Tossed with Sweet and Stingin' Honey Mustard Dressing. "Dr. Livingstone, I presume?"

THE ISLANDER V £6.95
A mammoth Caesar style salad. "A feast in itself."
Topped with grilled, marinated chicken add 75p

GARDEN OF EDEN V £6.75
Mounded mixed baby greens tossed with our Paradise Balsamic Vinaigrette Dressing and topped with chopped, marinated tomatoes and crostini bread.
Topped with grilled, marinated chicken add 75p
Topped with sautéed shrimp add £1.00

CHINA ISLAND CHICKEN SALAD £9.45
Shredded lettuce, tender grilled chicken breast, rice noodles, toasted sesame seeds potato sticks, shredded carrots and chopped shallots. Tossed lightly and piled high with our signature China Island Salad Dressing. "Chop! Chop!"

sandwiches

THE PLANT SANDWICH V £8.45
A humongous grilled mushroom with zucchini, roasted red peppers and fresh spinach. Nestled on a bed of Romaine lettuce tossed with our fabulous Caesar Extraordinaire Dressing and served on a multigrain bun.

RUMBLE IN THE JUNGLE £7.95
Romaine lettuce tossed with Caesar Extraordinaire Dressing topped with sliced turkey and stuffed into warm grilled pitta bread. Served with Roma tomatoes and cranberry relish and topped with crispy fried onions. "Can you feel the rumble?"

BLUE MOUNTAIN CHICKEN £8.55
6oz. tender, grilled chicken breast seasoned with our special spice, Captivating Cajun. Served with Rainforest Rescue Sauce on a toasted bun. "Chase away the blues!"
Topped with Swiss cheese add 50p

MAUI CHICKEN CLUB S £8.95
A tender, Cajun spiced grilled chicken breast, topped with roasted red peppers, bacon, Swiss cheese, lettuce, tomato and Rainforest Rescue Sauce. Served on granary bread.

GORILLA GRILLED CHEESE £6.55
Crisp bacon and fresh diced tomatoes served on thick cut grilled granary bread with melted Swiss and cheddar cheese. "Magilla's favourite!"

All sandwiches served with waffle fries

2 **Look at the *Rainforest Cafe* menu and answer these questions as quickly as you can.**

a How many salad dishes are there?
b How much is a *Rumble in the Jungle*?
c How many dishes cost £8.95?
d Which is the cheapest salad?
e How much is *The African Wind*?
f If you order a *Garden of Eden* and a *Gorilla Grilled Cheese*, how much do you spend?

Key language

Look at these sentences. They are often used to order food and drink in a restaurant.

Can I have an African Wind?
I'd like a Garden of Eden, *please*.
My friend would like an Islander, *and I'll have a* Plant Sandwich, *please*.

The waiter may ask you:
Would you like a salad?
Do you want a sandwich?

Now turn to page 78 for practice!

Talk about it

3 **Work in groups of three. One person is the waiter and the other two are customers. Look at the *Rainforest Cafe* menu and decide what to have.**
When you are ready, give the waiter your order.
Begin like this:

Waiter	Good evening. Are you ready to order?
Customer 1	Yes. Can I have ... ?
Customer 2	I'd like a ...

4 **The *Rainforest Cafe* is a so-called theme restaurant. The idea is to give customers an 'experience', rather than just a meal.**
Work with a partner and discuss these questions.

- Would you go to the *Rainforest Cafe*? Why? Why not?
- Are there any theme restaurants in your country?
- If yes. Have you visited any of them? If no, do you think they would be popular in your country?
- Imagine you are designing a theme restaurant. What would be your theme? For example: cinema, sport

Write about it

5 **Find out what kinds of restaurant are near you. Are there any unusual restaurants, like the *Rainforest Cafe*, or ones from different countries?**
What kind of food do they serve?
Which would you like to visit and why?
Begin like this:

In ... there are ... restaurants.
The ... restaurant is unusual because ...
There are also ... and ...

Born Free?

Tune in

1 Before you listen. Do you like zoos? Have you ever been to a zoo? What did you like/dislike about it?

2 Listen to the interviews with Dawn and Rory about zoos. Write in the spaces below who likes zoos and who does not. Then, listen again and write down four reasons each person gives. The first one has been done for you.

Zoos can be fun for people, but what about the animals?

Dawn .... zoos

Reasons why:

1 *people can see some fantastic animals*

2 ....

....

3 ....

....

4 ....

....

Rory .... zoos

Reasons why:

1 ....

....

2 ....

....

3 ....

....

4 ....

....

to breed to mate animals so as to increase their numbers

in captivity not free - in a zoo or park

to die out to become extinct

natural habitat the place where an animal lives in the wild

to get the chance to have the opportunity

to abolish to officially end an activity or thing

a breeding programme a programme to increase the numbers of an animal

Key language

Look at these ways of asking for and giving an opinion.

- **Asking for an opinion**
  Do you think we should still have zoos?
- **Giving an opinion**
  If you ask me, zoos are just for making money.
  In my view, I don't think you can learn much about animals in zoos.
  Personally, I think/don't think they are much fun for the animals.
- **Agreeing with an opinion**
  I agree with Dawn.
- **Disagreeing with an opinion**
  I disagree with that idea.

Now turn to page 78 for practice!

Do killer whales enjoy doing tricks?

Sounds like this!

3 Listen carefully to the following expressions from the *Key language*. Mark the words in each sentence which are stressed. The first one has been done for you.

Do you think ...?	*Personally, I think ...*
I think ...	*I agree with ...*
If you ask me, ...	*I disagree with ...*
In my view, ...	

Now listen again and repeat.

Talk about it

4 There are plans to open a *Sea World* in your town: whales, dolphins, sharks and seals will live there and perform for the public. Decide whether you are for or against the project. Write down your reasons.

Then, work in small groups and share your opinions on the *Sea World* project. How many people in your group shared your views?

Write about it!

5 Everyone in your town is talking about the *Sea World* project. You feel very strongly about it and decide to write to the Letters page of your local newspaper, *The Star*.

Use the letter below as a model.

5, Vine Road
Harlow
Essex
3rd July

The Editor
The Star
Harlow

Dear Sir,

There are plans to build a Sea World in our town and I am writing to explain why I am for/against the project.

First of all, I think that ... , because ...
Secondly, ...

I look forward to reading other people's views on this matter.

Yours faithfully,

Focus

1 Before you read. The blockbuster film *Titanic*, told of the tragic events of April 14th 1912, when the luxury liner hit an iceberg and sank, killing 1,523 people.

Read about it

2 How did the disaster happen? Read the text and note down three events which contributed to the tragedy.

Countdown to tragedy

Sunday 14th April
Morning

The *Titanic* was sailing from Southampton to New York. It was the fourth day of her maiden voyage. Bruce Ismay of the White Star Line, the ship's owners, was sailing on the ship. Ismay wanted to arrive in New York a day early and he asked the Captain to increase the ship's speed. The Captain was unhappy, but he agreed. The ship's speed was increased to 21.5 knots.

9.40 pm

The *Titanic*'s wireless operator was working alone, when he received a message from another ship, the *Mesaba*, warning of icebergs in the area. The operator was busy sending and receiving passengers' messages and he did not pass the *Mesaba's* warning to the Captain.

11.00 pm

It was a cold, moonless night. The lookouts were keeping watch, but they weren't using binoculars - the ship's pair were missing.

The first and second-class passengers were relaxing after dinner. The Captain was not on the bridge. He was getting ready for bed in his cabin.

11.37 pm

The two lookouts spotted a huge iceberg. It was about 500 metres in front of the *Titanic*. They telephoned the bridge with the message: 'Iceberg dead ahead.' The Quartermaster spun the ship's wheel as fast as he could. But it was too late. The ship was sailing too fast, and was too big to change direction quickly.

11.40 pm

The *Titanic* hit the iceberg. The ship shook, but most of the passengers were sleeping and were not disturbed.

The Chief Stoker was inspecting the boiler room after the collision, when he saw water pouring through a gash in the ship's hull. The tragedy of the *Titanic* was about to unfold.

a maiden voyage the first time a ship sails

a wireless operator a person responsible for sending and receiving radio messages

the lookouts sailors whose job it is to watch for obstacles in a ship's path

(a pair of) binoculars an instrument that you look through to see distant objects

the Quartermaster the officer on the bridge who is in charge of steering the ship

the hull the 'body' of a ship

a gash a deep cut

3 Read the text again and answer these questions.

a How many people died in the disaster?
b Why was the ship sailing so fast?
c Why didn't the wireless operator pass the *Mesaba's* message to the Captain?
d What were the passengers doing at 11.00 pm?
e Why didn't the lookouts see the iceberg sooner?
f Why didn't the *Titanic* turn away from the iceberg in time?

Key language

Look at these sentences.

Bruce Ismay was sailing on the Titanic.
Most of the passengers were sleeping.
subject + *was/were* + verb + *'ing'*

The Captain wasn't on the bridge.
The lookouts weren't using binoculars.
subject + *was/were (n't)* + verb + *'ing'* + object

What was the captain doing at 11.00 pm?
Were the passengers sleeping?
was/were + subject + verb + *'ing'?*

These are examples of the past continuous. We use it to talk about actions in progress at a time in the past.
We often use it to talk about longer, 'background' activities in the past which were interrupted.
For example: *Most of the passengers were asleep, when the ship hit the iceberg.*

Now turn to page 79 for practice!

Talk about it

4 **What were you, your family or friends doing at 9.30 last night? Make notes about each person's activities, then tell your partner. Begin like this:**

A What were you doing at 9.30 last night?
B Well, I was ...
A What was your father doing?
B He was ..., and my mother was ...
What about you?

5 **Work in groups of four and discuss the statements below.**

- Films like *Titanic* help people to understand historical events.
- The makers of *Titanic* just wanted to make money out of a terrible tragedy.
- *Titanic* cost $200 million. It is wrong to spend so much money on making a film.

Write about it

6 **Imagine you were one of the lookouts on board the *Titanic* the night of the tragedy. Write about what you saw and what you did that night.**
Begin like this:

It was a cold, moonless night.
We were ...

A film crew on location

Tune in

1 Before you listen. Look at the film titles below and match them with the correct film type from the box. The first one has been done for you.

- **Grease** ☐ *musical*
- **Elizabeth** ☐ ....
- **Interview with the Vampire** ☐ ....
- **Terminator** ☐ ....
- **Four Weddings and a Funeral** ☐ ....
- **Mulan** ☐ ....
- **Star Wars** ☑ ....
- **Funny Bones** ☐ ....
- **A Perfect Murder** ☐ ....

horror	thriller	action
romance	cartoon	science fiction
comedy	costume drama	musical

2 Listen to these people talking about films and tick (✓) the types you hear above. The first one has been done for you.

3 Now listen again and answer these questions.

a What did Sandy like about *Titanic*?
b What did David like about *Star Wars*?
c Why did Abbie like *There's Something about Mary*?
d What did Abbie like about *Mouse Hunt*?
e Who did Abbie think was the best actor in *Mouse Hunt*?
f Why did Sandy like *The Man in the Iron Mask*?

Key language

Look at these ways of talking about films.

- **Starting the conversation**

  Tell me about your favourite film.
  What's your favourite film about?

- **Giving your opinions**

  I really liked Titanic. *It had everything.*
  I didn't like Titanic *at all.*
  The costumes *were* amazing/dull.
  The special effects *were* fantastic/terrible.
  The acting *was* brilliant/awful.
  It was really funny/exciting/boring.
  I thought there was too much romance.

- **Talking about your preferences**

  I prefer action *films.*
  I'm not really keen on films like Terminator.
  I like comedy *films best.*

Now turn to page 79 for practice!

Sounds like this!

4 **Listen to these adjectives from the *Key language*. Mark the stressed syllable. The first one has been done for you.**

amazing	*fantastic*	*terrible*	*dull*	*funny*
awful	*exciting*	*boring*	*brilliant*	

Listen again and repeat.

Listen and repeat these sentences from the *Key language*. Try to copy the speaker's stress and intonation.

I really liked Titanic.

I didn't like Titanic *at all.*

The costumes were amazing.

The special effects were fantastic.

It was really exciting.

Talk about it

5 **Work in pairs. Talk about your favourite films.**
Begin like this:

A Tell me about your favourite film, *(name)*.
B Well, my favourite film is ...
The main actors were ...
The film was about ...
I really liked the ...
The ... were ...
What's your favourite film, *(name)*?

Have you seen any good films lately?

Write about it

6 **Imagine you are a film reviewer for *The Daily Star* newspaper. Write a review about a film you have seen, either at the cinema or on TV. Use the notes below to help you. Then write your review in a paragraph.**

Name of film: ....
Type of film: ....
The stars: ....
What the film was about: ....
My opinions of the film: ....
Marks out of ten for the film: .../10

Focus

1 **Before you read. Who is your favourite sports star? What sport does he/she play? Tell another student.
In pairs, make a list in English of as many sports as you can. For example: football, athletics**

Read about it

Young, sporting and rich

Sport today means big business for both players and sponsors. Sporting events like the World Cup, which has a TV audience of 35 billion people, make huge amounts of money. Companies like Coca Cola and Adidas have paid more than $20 million to sponsor a sports event. They know that people all over the world will see their names and logos at the sports stadiums and on participants' clothes.

Today, very few sportsmen are truly amateur. Many top stars, both 'amateur' and professional, make a fortune during their sporting careers. In fact, sportsmen say that they need to earn a lot of money because their careers are so short.

Tiger Woods, the professional golfer, is only 23 years old. He has already earned more than $5 million. He has won eight tournaments in his career so far, including the US Masters which he won in 1997. He reached the position of the world's top player in the shortest time ever - just 42 weeks. He is sponsored by Nike, the sportswear company.

Michael Jordan, the American basketball star who retired in 1999, was the world's richest player. In his last season he earned $34 million. Sponsorship earned him about ten times his salary.

Coca Cola sponsor large sporting events.

Today, there is a lot of pressure on young stars to do better and better in their sport. The high rewards have encouraged some sportsmen to take drugs to improve their performance. In 1998, the popular American athletics champion, Florence Griffiths-Joyner, died of heart failure.
She was 38. Some newspapers said that her death was related to the drugs she had taken during her athletics career. Is this the way sport should be?

events *(in this context)* sports meetings, games
to sponsor *(in this context)* to invest money in a sports event or athlete in exchange for advertising a product or name
to make a fortune to earn a lot of money
to retire *(in this context)* to stop competing in a sport
valuable worth a lot of money
to promote *(in this context)* to give publicity to a name or product
pressure influence, force

2 **Look at the text and find the answers to these questions as quickly as you can.**

a Why do sports people say they need to earn a lot of money?
b How much has Tiger Woods earned ?
c How many tournaments has he won?
d How much did Michael Jordan earn in his last season?
e Why do some athletes take drugs?

Key language

Look at these sentences.

He has won eight tournaments in his career so far. (His career is not over.)

They have sponsored a lot of events. (They still sponsor events.)

subject + *have/has* + past participle of verb + object

She hasn't taken drugs.

subject + *have/has* + not (*n't*) + past participle of verb + object

Has he earned a lot of money?
Yes, he has./No, he hasn't.

have/has + subject + past participle + object?

These are examples of the present perfect. It is used to describe actions and situations which started in the past and continue up to the present time.
In regular verbs, the past participle is the same as the simple past form of the verb: *earn, earned, earned.*

Now turn to page 80 for practice!

Talk about it

3 **Make a list of things you have done in your life so far. Make sure you know the past participles of the verbs you need. For example: learned to swim, passed my exams, won a school prize**
Tell another student about your achievements. Begin like this:

A What have you done in your life so far?
B Well, I've ... and I've ...
What about you?

Write about it

4 **Find out about a famous sports personality and write a paragraph about him/her. Use the notes below to help you.**

Name:
Nationality:
Sport:
Who he/she plays for, or represents:
Medals, records, prizes:
Sponsors:

Tiger Woods

Tune in

1 Before you listen. Do you like football? If yes, which team do you support? Have you ever been to a football match?

2 Listen to the street interviews and tick (✓) whether each of the three speakers has been to a football match or not.

Name	Yes	No
Jane	....	....
Vijay	....	....
Steve	....	....

3 Check your answers with a partner. Begin like this:

A Jane hasn't been to a football match. Is that right?

B Yes, that's right./No, that's wrong.

Scottish football fans enjoying a game.

loads of *(slang)* lots of

violence aggressive behaviour where people get hurt

ever at any time, at any point in your life

never not at any time, not at any point in your life

fighting when two or more people hit each other

supporters fans

atmosphere mood or tone of a place or a situation

Key language

Look at these sentences.

I've never been to a football match.
We've never seen any violence.

Never is a time adverb and it is used in affirmative sentences. It means 'not at any time so far.'

Have you ever been to a football match?
Yes, I have./No, I haven't.
Has Vijay ever seen any violence?
Yes, he has./No, he hasn't.

Ever is used in questions to ask about someone's experiences. It means 'at any time so far'.

Now turn to page 80 for practice!

Sounds like this!

4 **Listen and repeat these sentences. Try to copy the speaker's stress and intonation.**

Has he ever been to a football match?
Yes, he has.
No, he hasn't.
I've never seen any violence.

Talk about it

5 **Find out about your classmates' experiences. Look at this list of questions, then write three more of your own. When you are ready, interview three people in your class.**

- Have you ever been to a football match?
- Have you ever met a famous person?
- Have you ever won a competition?
- Have you ever ....?
- Have you ever ....?
- Have you ever ....?

What were the two most interesting experiences you talked about?

Canoe clubs are very popular.

Violence has given British soccer a bad name.

6 **Work in groups of four and share your opinions on the questions below.**

Do you think that:

- anything can be done about violence at football matches?
- alcohol should be sold to supporters before a game?
- footballers are paid too much money?
- people take football too seriously?
- football should be sponsored?

Write about it

7 **Write about a sport that you enjoy doing, or are interested in. Write about your involvement in the sport.**
For example: whether you play on a team, belong to a club, or go to events.
Then, write about any sporting ambitions you have.
Begin like this:

I am very interested in ... because ...
I particularly like/enjoy ... and ...
I play .../belong to a ... club/go to events ...
I would like to ... in the future.

Focus

1 Before you read. Have you got a mobile phone? How many people you know have got one?

Read about it

2 What was life like before mobile phones were invented? It's hard to imagine! Since they were introduced in 1985, ten million people in Britain have bought one. Read what these people say about them. Who uses a mobile phone?

Andy

"Mobile phones are just everywhere! I bought mine last year. They can be really useful, but at times they are very irritating! The other day I was listening to a lecture, when somebody's mobile phone started ringing. Some places, like restaurants, have banned mobile phones, and I think that's a good thing."

Karen

"I just love my mobile phone! I can call friends whenever I want to! But my phone is useful too. The other night, I missed the last bus home. I called my Mum on my mobile and she came to pick me up in her car. Thank goodness I have a mobile! It makes me feel safer."

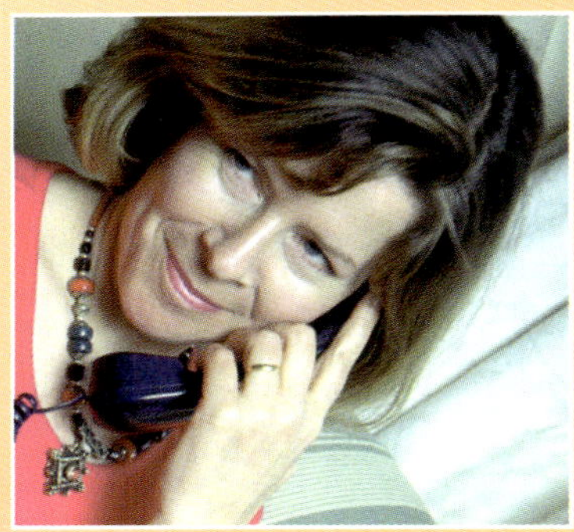

Tara

"I'm not sure about mobiles. Some scientists are saying they are not safe and can cause brain tumours. I was thinking about having one, but I've changed my mind now. You can always find a phone box if you really need to make a call."

3 Read these sentences and decide whether they are true or false. Correct the false ones.

a Mobile phones were first introduced in 1995.

b Ten million people in Britain have bought a mobile phone.

c Andy likes mobile phones.

d Karen feels safer when she is carrying a mobile phone.

e Some scientists believe mobile phones can make you ill.

f Tara wants a mobile phone now.

a mobile phone a small telephone you can carry around with you

irritating annoying, causing anger

to ban to disallow an activity

to miss a bus to arrive at a bus stop after the bus has left

to pick (someone) up to collect someone

Thank goodness! an expression used when you are grateful for something

to change (one's) mind to change your opinions about something

Key language

Look at these sentences.

The other night, I missed the last bus home. (simple past)
Some places have banned mobile phones. (present perfect)

We use the simple past to talk about past events which happened in finished periods of time: *the other night, last year*. The event is not connected to the present time.
We use the present perfect to talk about past events which have a present result. *Some places have banned mobile phones*. (You cannot use a mobile phone there now.)

Now turn to page 81 for practice!

Talk about it

4 **Work in pairs. Share your opinions on the following statements.**

- Mobile phones are irritating. People should not be allowed to use them in public places.
- Mobile phones are an essential part of life, like computers.
- Mobile phones are a fashion accessory and are not really necessary.

Write about it

5 **Choose a modern invention.**
For example: the internet, personal stereos
Make a list of the good points and the bad points of the invention. Then, write about them. Begin like this:

The Internet is a useful invention because ...
It also ...
However, there are some disadvantages.
Firstly, ...
Secondly,
Personally, I think the internet is ...

Mobile phone users can be a nuisance in public places.

Do your parents complain about your telephone calls?

Tune in

1 **Before you listen. Do you enjoy chatting on the phone? Are your conversations long or short?**

2 **Listen to the three telephone conversations and answer these questions.**

a Who wants to speak to Mike?
b Is Mike at home?
c Who wants to speak to Françoise?
d Is Françoise at home?
e What's Roberto's phone number?
f What's Maria's phone number?

Key language

Look at these expressions we use when talking on the telephone.

- **Checking you have the right number**
  Is that 440379?
- **Asking to speak to someone**
  Is Janette *there, please?*
  Can I speak to Dave, *please?*
- **Passing the call to the right person**
  Hang on a moment, Ross. *I'll just get* him.
- **Saying someone is not at home**
  I'm afraid she's *not here at the moment.*
- **Offering to take a message**
  Can I take a message?
- **Asking to leave a message**
  Can I leave a message?
- **Giving a message**
  Can you tell her Roberto *called?*
  Can you ask him *to call me back?*
- **Promising to give the message**
  I'll give her *your message.*

Now turn to page 81 for practice!

Sounds like this!

3 Listen and repeat the expressions from the *Key language*. Try to copy the speaker's stress and intonation.

Talk about it

4 Work in pairs. Decide who is to be the parent and who is to be Pete. Read your role card and prepare your part.

Parent
Your daughter Cathy gets a lot of phone calls! She isn't at home this evening - she is playing basketball for her college. Take a phone message from her friend.

Pete
You are a college friend of Cathy's. You are having problems with your Economics homework and you need to speak to Cathy urgently! Leave a message for her.

When you are both ready, begin like this:

Parent Hello, 921683.
Pete Hello. Is Cathy there, please?

Write about it

5 Write a telephone conversation between an ex-boyfriend and girlfriend. Before you start, think about the reasons for the telephone conversation and what the outcome will be.
Begin like this:

Lee *Hello, 02564.*
Sandy *Hi, Lee. It's Sandy. There's something we need to talk about. ...*

6 When you have finished, act out your dialogue with a partner.

Dear Tracey...

Focus

1 Before you read. If you have a problem, who do you go to for advice? For example: a parent

Read about it

2 Read these problems from a teenage magazine. What sort of problems are they?

Tracey's here to help!

Write to Tracey!

Boyfriends, girlfriends, parents and exams - just a few of the problems you cope with every day. Sure, growing up is exciting, but it has its agonies too! So, if you have a problem, write to Tracey and share it!

Dear Tracey,

I am 17 years old and will be taking my A levels next year and I hope to go to university. My problem is that my parents are always arguing and now, my mother is talking about a divorce! This is making me feel very depressed. I don't feel I have anyone to talk to at school, as all my friends are so busy with their studies or their girlfriends. At times I think I should give up school and run away from home.

What's your advice?

Dan

Dear Dan,

It is hard when parents divorce, but yours might just be having a few problems right now. You shouldn't run away from home - your parents love you, and life alone can be very difficult. Tell your parents exactly how you feel and how upset you are. You shouldn't give up your studies, but explain to them that you are finding it difficult to work with all the problems at home. I am sure your friends will be very supportive, once they know what is happening in your life - you should talk to them, too.

Tracey

Dear Tracey,

My best friend, Karen, has started going out with Richard, who seems a really nice guy. The only problem is, I have found out that he has got a girlfriend already! And, the girlfriend is a girl from our school! All his friends are laughing about it. I know Karen will be very upset if I tell her, but what should I do?

Nicky

Dear Nicky,

This is a tricky problem! Perhaps you should talk to Richard first and see if it is true that he has another girlfriend. If it is true, then he should be honest with Karen and tell her. He might not want to do this. In which case, why don't you tell Karen yourself? After all, you are her best friend!

Tracey

advice an opinion you give someone about a problem

agonies problems, troubles

a divorce the legal ending of a marriage

depressed sad, miserable

upset unhappy, worried

to give up (something) to stop doing something

tricky difficult

3 Read the text again and complete these sentences.

a Dan is feeling depressed because ....

b Tracey thinks that Dan should ....

c Tracey says Dan shouldn't run .... because ....

d Nicky is worried because ....

e Tracey says Nicky should .... first.

f If Richard doesn't want to talk to Karen, then Nicky should ....

Key language

Look at these sentences.

You should talk to Richard first.
You shouldn't run away from home.

subject + *should (n't)* + verb infinitive + object

What should I do?
Should I tell my friend? — *Yes, you should. /No, you shouldn't.*

We use *should* to ask for and give advice. It is a modal verb, like *will*, *could* and *might*. (See page 27.)

Now turn to page 82 for practice!

Sounds like this!

4 **Listen to these sentences. Notice that the *'l'* in *should* is not pronounced.**

What should I do?
Should I tell my friend?
You shouldn't give up your studies.
He should be honest with Karen.

Now listen again and repeat.

Talk about it

5 **Work with a partner. Read the problems below and decide what advice you would give to each person. Begin like this:**

A I think Marie should ...
B Yes, that's a good idea. She should also ... /No. I think she should ...

I'm worried about my best friend. She doesn't eat breakfast or lunch any more and she is getting very thin. When I talk to her about this, she says she is fat! What should I do to help her?
Marie

My parents got divorced last year. Now my Mum wants to marry her new boyfriend! I don't like him at all! Should I ask her not to marry him?
Pete

Trouble in the family

Write about it

6 Invent a problem and write a letter to Tracey. When you have finished, exchange letters with another student and write an answer to their problem.

Tune in

1 Before you listen. Make a list in English of family members. For example: brother, aunt
Compare your list with a partner.

2 Listen to Tomoko and Zeeshan talking about teenage life in their communities. Tomoko is from Japan and Zeeshan is a British Muslim. Tick (✓) the family members they mention on your list.

Tomoko

Zeeshan

3 Now listen again and answer these questions.

a Where does Tomoko live?
b Are her parents strict?
c When do teenagers start dating in Japan?
d Does Zeeshan live at home?
e What does Zeeshan say about family parties?
f What does Zeeshan say about dating in his community?

strict someone who expects rules to be obeyed

to get on (with someone) to have a good relationship (with someone)

to be allowed (to do something) to be permitted

dating when boys and girls go out together romantically

to socialise to spend time with people in a friendly way

religion a belief in God or gods. Christianity and Islam are two religions

Key language

Look at these questions.

Do you live at home?
Do you get on with your parents?
Are your parents strict?
Are you allowed to have boyfriends/girlfriends/parties?
When do people start dating in Japan?
How do you meet girls/boys?

Now turn to page 82 for practice!

Talk about it

4 **Interview another student. Ask him/her about her family life and what he/she is allowed to do. Use the questions in the *Key language* to help you.**
Begin like this:

A Tell me about your family.
B I live with my ... We live in ...
A Do you get on with your parents?

What's your family like?

5 **Do you agree with these statements? Share your opinions with a partner.**

- Teenagers shouldn't start dating until they are 16 years old.
- Your parents are the best people to choose your husband/wife.
- Teenagers should tell their parents about their problems.
- Teenagers these days have too much freedom.

Write about it

6 **Write about your family and your relationship with your parents. Use the model below on the right to help you.**

My name is ... I am ... years old.
I live with my ...
My ... are strict about ...

At weekends, I am allowed to ...,
but I am not allowed to ...

My friends and I usually ...
I am/not allowed to have
boyfriends/girlfriends, but ...

People usually start dating in ... when
they are about ... years old.

Focus

1 **Before you read. When was the last time you went to the doctor's? What was wrong with you? What treatment did you receive?**

Read about it

2 **Medicine has made many advances in the last 100 years. Common remedies then seem barbaric to us today! Bloodletting was probably one of the most gruesome. Where did bloodletting take place?**

Bloodletting in1804

What was bloodletting?

Bloodletting (draining the blood from the body) was an important treatment for a wide range of diseases for many years. Surgeons used to make cuts on the patient's body and drain the blood into little bowls. This might seem a strange way to cure illnesses to us, but in the past doctors believed in it. Surgeons often collected between one and four pints of blood (over two litres), and they did not stop until the patient fainted.
George Washington, the first President of the United States, died in 1799 after doctors drained nine pints of blood from him in one day! All he had complained of was a throat infection!

Where did people go for treatment?

In those days people did not always go to their doctor for this type of treatment. A barber could do it for them! Barbers did not just cut hair - they were also surgeons. They used to pull people's teeth out, if they had toothache. (Of course, they didn't use to give patients anaesthetic in those days!) That is why the traditional barber's shop sign is a red and white-striped pole - red for blood, white for bandages.

When did surgeons stop bloodletting?

Surgeons practised bloodletting until the nineteenth century. In fact, even as late as 1923, Sir William Osler recommended it in his book *Principles and Practices of Medicine*. Fortunately, the only cut you will get from a barber's shop today is a hair cut!

surgeons doctors who perform operations

to drain to empty (a liquid)

a barber a man who cuts men's hair

anaesthetic a drug to make a patient unconscious

to faint to lose consciousness for a short time

a throat infection a minor disease inside your neck

toothache pain in the tooth

3 **Read the text again and decide whether these statements are true or false. Correct the false ones.**

a Bloodletting used to be an important form of treatment.
b Surgeons made just one cut on the patient's body.
c They only collected a little blood.
d George Washington died of a throat infection.
e Only doctors used to practise bloodletting.
f Some doctors still recommended bloodletting in the twentieth century.

Key language

Look at these sentences.

Barbers used to pull people's teeth out.
They didn't use to give patients anaesthetic.
Where did people use to go for treatment?

Notice the differences between the affirmative, negative and interrogative forms of *used to*.

We use *used to* when we want to talk about things people often did in the past. We do not use it to talk about things people only did once.

Compare

Surgeons used to collect blood in small bowls. (past habit)
Doctors collected nine pints of blood from George Washington. (only once)

Now turn to page 83 for practice!

Sounds like this!

4 **Listen carefully to how *used to* is pronounced in these sentences from the *Key language*.**

Now listen again and repeat.

Talk about it

5 **How was life different in your country a hundred years ago? In groups, talk about the things people used to and didn't use to do. Use the topics below to help you.**

- transport
- work
- family life
- machines

Begin like this:

A A hundred years ago in my country, people used to walk to work. People didn't have cars then.

B Yes. People used to walk a lot more then.

Cheapside London, 1902

Write about it

6 **Now write about the things you discussed in the *Talk about it* activity. Which changes do you think have made life better for people? Have any changes made life worse?**

Tune in

1 **Before you listen. In Britain, treatments such as acupuncture and osteopathy have become very popular. These are called alternative therapies, as they are different from conventional, science-based medicine. Are alternative therapies used in your country?**

2 **Here are some of the alternative therapies that are used in Britain. Match the word on the left with its definition on the right.**

i **iridology**	a treatment which uses massage and perfumed oils
ii **homeopathy**	b moving the patient's bones and muscles to treat pain
iii **aromatherapy**	c treating a disease with a substance which actually causes the disease
iv **osteopathy**	d looking at the patient's eyes to discover what is wrong

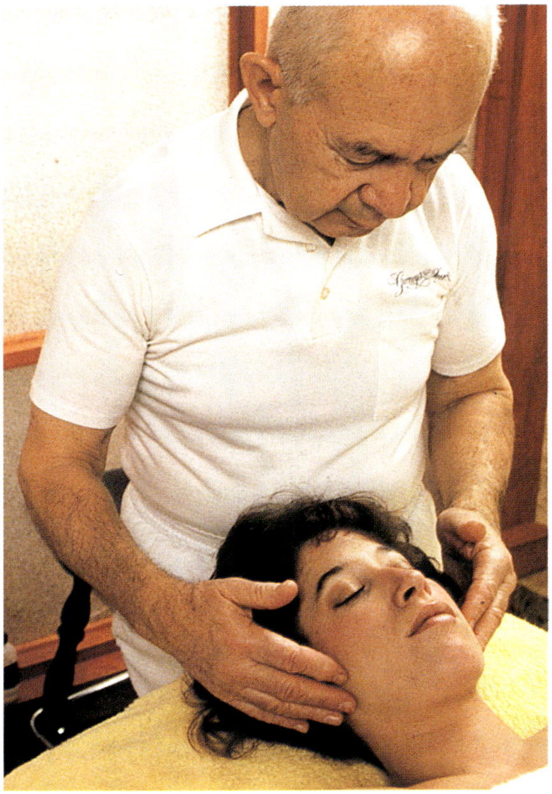

An aromatherapist

to diagnose to discover what is wrong with a patient
to accept *(in this context)* to agree with
symptoms signs of a disease which you can see or feel
side effects the negative effects of taking a medicine
stress tension, anxiety
pain relief treatment to stop pain
to channel to move something in one direction

3 **Now listen to Ian Stanley, President of the Alternative Therapy Society of Great Britain, giving a talk on the future of alternative medicine. Listen and check your definitions above. One of the therapies is not mentioned. Which?**

4 **Listen again and complete these sentences.**

a Ian Stanley says that alternative therapies will be used ...
  i in the place of Western medicine.
  ii together with Western medicine.

b Iridology will help ...
  i discover a patient's disease.
  ii cure a patient's disease.

c Homeopathy ...
  i cures the symptoms of the disease.
  ii uses medicines to produce the symptoms of the disease.

d New technology sometimes ...
  i has side effects on the patient.
  ii does not work.

e Aromatherapy ...
  i can cause stress.
  ii helps you to relax.

Key language

Look at these sentences.

Medicine will be very different.

Doctors won't use drugs all the time.

subject + *will (n't)* + verb infinitive + object

How will medicine change in the future?

question word + *will* + subject + verb infinitive?

We use *will* when we want to make predictions about the future. If we are less sure about our predictions, we can use *could* or *might*.

Patients might have fewer operations in the future. (See page 27.)

Now turn to page 83 for practice!

Talk about it

5 **Think about the next 100 years. How will medicine and our health change? Look at the topics below and make predictions.**

- men having babies
- human clones
- life expectancy
- people's health, generally
- serious illnesses such as cancer and heart disease

When you are ready, work with a partner. Read out your predictions. Your partner should agree or disagree with them.

Begin like this:

A Men will have babies in a hundred years' time.

B Rubbish! Men won't have babies! /Yes, I think you're right.

6 **Discuss these questions with a partner.**

- Have you ever had any alternative therapy?
- Do you think alternative therapies are useful to modern medicine?

Is this how babies will be made in the future?

Have a nose job

Focus

1 Before you read. Make a list of famous people who have had cosmetic surgery. For example: Cher, Michael Jackson What parts of their bodies have they changed?

Michael Jackson

Read about it

2 Now read the article about Sammy. What part of her body does she want to change?

Sammy is 11 years old. She is young, healthy and attractive. But for some reason, she is not happy with her looks. 'When I grow up, I'm going to be a singer or a dancer. It's hard to get into show business. Looks are important and I'm going to do everything I can to become famous. I'm saving all my pocket money so I can have a nose job for my sixteenth birthday.'

Sammy's mum, who is an actress, agrees. 'Sammy's nose is OK now, but by the time she's a teenager, it'll be enormous - like mine was at her age. If Sammy has a big nose, she won't make it in show business. If she wants cosmetic surgery, then she can have it.'

Dr Steve Harding, a child psychologist, says: 'Sammy is a good-looking kid, but she thinks she is going to need a nose job to succeed. I say, look at those stars who have made it in spite of their noses - Barbra Streisand, Gerard Depardieu. The problem with cosmetic surgery is that patients are never satisfied. First it's their nose, then it's their eyes or something else. People can easily attach their life problems to their so-called physical defects. But surgery can't change the person you are inside.'

cosmetic surgery an operation to change your face or body to make it look more attractive

looks physical appearance

show business the entertainment industry: cinema, theatre

pocket money money that parents give to their children

a nose job *(slang)* cosmetic surgery to make your nose more attractive

enormous very big

physical defects imperfections and faults of the body

3 **Read the text again and answer these questions.**

a What is Sammy going to do when she is 16?

b Why is she going to have cosmetic surgery?

c Does her mother agree or disagree with Sammy's decision?

d Does the child psychologist agree with Sammy's decision?

e Does he think a nose job is necessary to succeed in show business?

f What can't cosmetic surgery change?

Key language

Look at these sentences.

I'm going to be a singer or a dancer when I grow up.
subject + *be* + *going to* + infinitive without *to* + object

I'm not going to have a nose job until I am 16.
subject + *be* + *not* + *going to* + infinitive without *to* + object

What's Sammy going to do when she is 16?
'wh' + *be* + subject + *going to* + infinitive without *to* + object?

These are examples of the *going to* future form. We use it to talk about future intentions or things we have already decided to do. (Compare with *will* on page 17.)

Now turn to page 84 for practice!

Talk about it

4 **Make a list of your resolutions, and plans for the year ahead. For example: learn to ski, pass my exams, not be unkind to my little brother**
When you are ready. Tell a partner about them. For example:

A Tell me about your resolutions and plans.
B Well, I'm going to learn to ski in the next year, and I'm going to try to pass my exams. I'm not going to be unkind to my little brother.
What about you?

Learning to ski is very 'in'.

5 **Discuss these questions with a partner.**

- Do you think teenagers should be allowed to have cosmetic surgery?
- Do you think people should have to pay for cosmetic surgery?
- If you could change one part of your face, what would it be? Why?

Write about it

6 **Imagine you are Sammy's older brother or sister. Write about Sammy's ambitions and what she is going to do. Then say whether you agree or disagree with her decision.**

My sister Sammy is 11 years old.
She wants to be a ...
Sammy is going to have cosmetic surgery on her nose because ...
Personally, I think/don't think ... because ...

Have a nose job

Tune in

1 **Before you listen. Are you happy with the way you look? Do you worry about your appearance? Make a list of words associated with people's facial characteristics. Begin like this:**

hair	eyes	nose
blonde	*brown*	*small*
wavy		

Compare your list with a partner and add any new words to your list.

Dan

Magda

David

Anya

Jake

Tamsin

2 **Listen to these four interviews and tick (✓) the words on your list that you hear.**

3 **Now listen again and answer these questions.**

a What do Dan's friends worry about?
b What colour is Magda's hair at the moment?
c What does Anya think girls need?
d Does Anya worry about her looks?
e Why does Jake think that looks are a problem for girls more than boys?
f Does Jake think that looks are important?

(to be) on a diet to eat less food in order to lose weight

(one's) looks your physical appearance

to keep changing to change often

self-esteem positive feelings you have about yourself

a sense of humour an ability to enjoy a funny situation

fashion models men and women who wear clothes at fashion shows or in magazines

Key language

Look at these sentences.

I've got long, curly, blonde *hair.*
She's got, mousy *hair.*
They've both got nice figures.

We use *have/has got* for describing a person's appearance. (Compare *have got* on page 12.) *Have got* is followed by adjectives and then the noun they are describing. There are rules for the order of adjectives:

	1	2	3	4	
	opinion	length	type	colour	+ noun
She's got beautiful,		*long,*	*wavy,*	*dark*	*hair and blue eyes.*

Now turn to page 84 for practice!

Sounds like this!

4 **Listen and repeat these adjectives for describing peoples' hair. Check any you do not know in the *Word list*.**

long wavy straight blonde curly
fair frizzy dark short mousy

Talk about it

5 **Work in pairs. Look at the photos on page 56. Choose one and describe him/her to your partner. Do not give the person's name. Your partner must guess who it is. Take it in turns to describe each picture.**
Begin like this:

A It's a boy. He's got ... and ...
B Is it ...?
A Yes, it is./No, it isn't. Try again!

6 **Discuss these questions with your partner.**

- Looks are important.
- Teenagers must learn to feel good about themselves.
- Personality is more important than looks.
- Good-looking people choose good-looking partners.

Write about it

7 **You would like to join the *Two Hearts* dating agency and find your dream partner. Fill in the application form below and write a description of the person you would like to meet.**

Two Hearts

Name: ....

Age: ....

My dream partner: ....

....

....

....

....

....

....

....

Aliens!

Focus

1 Before you read. Is there life on other planets? Do you think creatures from outer space have visited Earth?

Read about it

2 Read this story about Jack, who believes he was kidnapped by aliens. Who kidnapped Jack?

'It's true I tell you! I thought I was going to die!' Jack is 45 years old. There is nothing strange about him, except that he believes he was kidnapped by aliens. I am Martin Blunt from CNB TV News, and I am here to talk to Jack about his experience.

'What happened?' I ask.

'I was driving home one night, when I saw some lights flashing in the sky. They moved towards me. Suddenly, my engine stopped. I got out of my car and stared. The flashing lights landed in front of me and two pink 'somethings' appeared. They were very small, had two legs and tiny heads.'

'Weren't you scared?'

'Sure I was scared!' he replies. 'I was taken into the spaceship by the two little creatures! I was put in a large, white room where I was examined by some kind of doctor. He seemed very interested in me.'

'What happened next?'

'Well, they all wanted to talk to me and I was asked a lot of questions.'

'How did you communicate?' I ask.

'Oh, there was a translator. I was told that they were studying different planets. I was even thanked for my help! Oh, one more thing! They told me where they came from - a planet called Earth. I've never heard of it before. I wonder where it is?'

I scratch my head with my tentacles and reply, 'I've no idea.'

An artist's impression of an alien as described by a witness.

3 Read the text again and answer these questions.

a What was Jack doing that night?
b What did Jack see?
c What did the aliens look like?
d Where did the aliens take Jack?
e What did the aliens do to Jack?
f Where did the aliens come from?

to be kidnapped to be captured and held against your will

aliens beings from other planets

creatures living things, animals

a spaceship a vehicle for travelling in space

scared afraid, frightened

examined looked at very closely

tentacles long, flexible arms, as on an octopus

Key language

Look at these sentences.

I was taken to their spaceship.
I was asked a lot of questions.
subject + *was/were* + past participle + object

These are examples of the past passive. We use the passive when we want to emphasise the action in a sentence, rather than the person who carried out the action. The past passive is used to describe past events which are finished.

Compare

The aliens asked me a lot of questions.
Who asked the questions, (the aliens) is important. This is an active sentence.
I was asked a lot of questions.
Who asked the questions is not important. This is a passive sentence.

Now turn to page 85 for practice!

Talk about it

4 **Work in pairs. One person is from Earth, the other is Jack, (who is from planet Zog). Read your role card and prepare your part.**

artner.

vel to

y

ship

as

The Earthling

Prepare questions to ask Jack about his world. Use the topics below to help you.

- the world he lives in
- his body
- what he eats
- how he spends his time

Day 17

We landed on planet ... at ... local time.
The planet was very strange. It ...
(describe the planet)

We found an alien. It said its name was Jack. It had ... (describe Jack)

We discovered that Jack ... (what did Jack tell you?)

Aliens!

Tune in

1 **Before you listen. Have you ever seen a UFO? Have you ever seen something strange which you could not explain?**

2 **Listen to George telling his friend Harry about a strange experience he had. Put the events below in the order you hear them. The first one has been done for you.**

a George phoned the police. ☐
b George's television stopped working. 1
c An alien spoke to George. ☐
d George woke up. ☐
e A UFO landed. ☐
f An alien shot George. ☐

Which of the events didn't you hear about?

3 **Now listen again and answer the questions.**

a Where does George live?
b Where did the UFO land?
c Who ran away?
d What did the aliens do to George?
e Did the police believe George?
f Does Harry believe George's story?

a UFO *(abbreviation)* an Unidentified Flying Object, an alien spaceship, for example
Calm down! an expression to make someone quieter
barking the loud noise a dog makes
spacesuits the clothes worn to travel in space
paralysed unable to move your body
kidding joking, not being serious
exhausted very tired

Key language

Look at these sentences.

I was watching TV, when the picture disappeared.
At first, I wasn't worried.
Meanwhile, Ben was barking like crazy.
Next, the door opened.
Then, they came into my house!
Much later, I woke up in the field.
Finally, I rang the police.

The underlined words and phrases on the left are 'linkers'. They are used to order the events in a story.

Put the underlined words in the correct column below, according to their meaning. The first one has been done for you.

'in the beginning'	'after'	'at the same time'	'at the end'
		when	

Now turn to page 85 for practice!

Sounds like this!

4 **Harry does not believe George's story. Listen and repeat these expressions Harry used to show this. Try to copy the speaker's stress and intonation.**

I don't believe you!
Never!
Oh come on, George!
You're kidding!
That can't be true!

Talk about it

6 **Work in groups of three and tell each other the stories you prepared in activity 5. Use the expressions from the *Sounds like this!* to show you do not believe the 'tall stories' you hear.**

Write about it

5 **George's story is difficult to believe. Such stories are called 'tall stories'. Write your own 'tall story', using the points below to help you. Remember to include some of the 'linkers' from the *Key language*.**

- Where and when did the story happen?
- Who was there and what did you see?
- What did you do?
- How did the story end?

When you have finished writing, prepare to tell your story.

That's a good story!

Uniformity?

Focus

1 Before you read. Imagine your parents are sending you to study at a school in London. Most schools in Britain have a uniform. How do you feel about wearing one?

Read about it

2 Now read what these London school students have to say about their uniforms. Which opinions do you agree with?

Kerry, 16

"If you come to my school, you'll have to wear a uniform just like mine - a skirt, blouse, tie and blazer in the school colours. Smart, isn't it?"

Phil, 17

"If you come to our school, you won't have to wear a uniform. We can wear what we like, within reason. Jeans and trainers are OK."

Nina, 14

"I think school uniform is a good idea because everyone looks the same. If you're rich or poor, it doesn't matter. Everyone looks equal."

Jez, 15

"If you wear a school uniform, you don't have to worry about what to wear every day."

Annie, 15

"If you like dark colours, you'll love my school uniform! Personally, I hate it! School uniforms are drab and old-fashioned!"

Emma, Maths teacher

"If pupils are wearing uniforms, then there is no peer pressure on them to wear the latest fashion. Everyone has to conform."

a uniform clothes which everyone in a school, or organisation wears
Uniformity everyone in a group looking the same
to vote to choose or decide something
it doesn't matter an expression to say that something is not important
drab dull and uninteresting
to conform to behave in the same way as others
peer pressure obligation to be the same as other people in a group

3 **Find the answers to these questions.**

a If you go to Kerry's school, what will you have to wear?
b What can you wear to Phil's school?
c Why is Nina in favour of school uniforms?
d Why does Jez like wearing a school uniform?
e What doesn't Annie like about her uniform?
f What does Emma say about school uniforms?

Key language

Look at these sentences.

If you come to my school, you'll have to wear a uniform like mine.
If you come to our school, you won't have to wear a uniform.
if + subject + present tense + object,
subject + *will* + verb infinitive + object

Will I have to wear a uniform, if I go to school in Britain?
will + subject + verb infinitive + object,
if + subject + present tense + object?

These are examples of the first conditional. (Compare with the zero conditional on page 7.) We use the first conditional to talk about real or possible situations and their results.

If you like dark colours, then you'll love my uniform!
(*if* clause = possible situation,
main clause = result)

Now turn to page 86 for practice!

Talk about it

4 **Work with a partner. Read the situations below and say what you would do in each.**

- there is nothing good on TV tonight
- it rains at the weekend
- you are late for school tomorrow
- you can't do your homework - it's too difficult

Begin like this:

A If there's nothing good on TV tonight, I'll ... And you?

5 **Discuss the following questions with your partner.**

- Do you think schools should have a uniform?
- Do you think teachers should wear a uniform?
- What would you like to wear to school tomorrow?

Write about it

6 **Describe your school uniform, or the clothes you usually wear to school. Use the example below as a model.**

At my school we have to/don't have to wear a uniform.

I wear .../My uniform consists of ...

Most school students in my country wear ... to go to school.

I would prefer to wear...

Uniformity?

1

2

3

4

5

6

Tune in

1 **Before you listen. Who wears a uniform in your country? Make a list. For example: the police, nurses**

2 **Match each photo with a job title from the list below.**

☐ *nurse* ☐ *pilot* ☐ *police officer* ☐ *fire fighter*
☐ *bank clerk* ☐ *soldier* ☐ *security guard* ☐ *cashier*

Some professions, like pilot or fire fighter, always have a uniform. Today, many companies want their staff to wear them, too. They say that uniforms make workers look smarter and feel part of a team.
Would you be happy to wear a uniform to work?
Now listen and tick (✓) whether the people on the right are for or against uniforms in the office.

Name	for	against
Nadia	....	....
Monag	....	....
Petra	....	....
Sara	....	....

3 **Listen again and complete the sentences below.**

a Nadia thinks staff in a bank look .... if they are wearing a uniform.
b Monag prefers people to look like individuals, not ....
c Petra would feel happier .... to work.
d Steve says that people wearing uniforms look more .... and businesslike.
e Sarah thinks that wearing a uniform in an office is ....
f Gill says if bosses want their workers to look smarter, they should ....

smart well-dressed, tidy
a clone an animal (or person) who is identical to another
personally in your opinion
businesslike efficient and practical
unnecessary not needed
employees the people who work for a company or organisation
bosses the managers in a company or organisation

Key language

Look at these sentences.

I'd feel happier wearing my own clothes.
I think the staff look better in a uniform.
They look smarter and more businesslike.

These are examples of comparative adjectives. We use them when we want to say that people or things are unequal in some way: *uniforms are smarter than ordinary clothes.*

To form the comparative of adjectives with one or two syllables add *'er'*: *smart*, *smarter.* Add *'ier'*, if the adjective ends in a *'y': pretty, prettier.* Add an *'r'* if the adjective ends in an *'e': nice*, *nicer*.

Sometimes the spelling changes: *fatter, bigger.*

In adjectives with more than two syllables, the comparative is formed by adding *more*: *more businesslike*, *more expensive.*

Some comparative adjectives are irregular: *good*, *better*: *bad*, *worse.*

Now turn to page 86 for practice!

Sounds like this!

4 **Put the adjectives below in the correct column depending on their comparative form. The first one has been done for you.**

happy smart serious expensive good big easy cheap nice businesslike reassuring

'r'	'er'	'ier'	more	irregular
		happier		

Listen and check your answers.

Talk about it

5 **Work with a partner. What would you wear to the following places?**

- an office where staff did not wear uniforms
- a school or college disco
- a job interview
- your grandmother's birthday party

It's difficult to decide what to wear!

Write about it

6 **Design a uniform for one of the following jobs. Think about who will wear the uniform and what the job involves. Draw your design and then write a description of it.**

- a nursery school teacher
- a shop assistant
- a builder
- a barman at a disco
- a gardener

Focus

1 **Before you read. Make a list of different types of crime.**
For example: murder, burglary
Compare your list with a partner.

Read about it

2 **Now read the text. What crimes are mentioned?**

If you thought crime only happened in Britain's cities, then you should think again. Margaret Cook was not mugged in London or Manchester, but in Exford, a small, provincial town in the south of England. There, as in many towns across Britain, crime is on the increase.

Many local people are scared to go out at night. Fifty-seven year-old Olive Mattocks says, 'The pubs in the town are partly to blame - if they didn't sell alcohol to under 18s, there wouldn't be so much trouble.'

Youth crime is a real problem. Half the criminals in Britain are under 21 years of age and 50 per cent of those are under 17. The average burglar is 17 years old.

Could boredom be a reason young people turn to crime? 'If young people had more things to do, there would be less crime in our town,' says policeman John Robinson. Rose Leach (45) adds, 'There wasn't much to do here when I was young either, but we made our own entertainment. Youngsters these days don't seem to be able to do that.'

Others, like Harry Richards (65), put the blame on low moral standards.

'I wouldn't dream of stealing or mugging someone. If young people knew the difference between right and wrong, there wouldn't be so much crime.'

Youths mug woman, 72

Teenage youths rampaging through the town centre, mugged 72 year-old Margaret Cook, who was on her way home from a shopping trip. The youths, who had just left the *Rose and Crown* pub on Queen Street ran through the town centre frightening shoppers and passers-by.

3 **Read the article again and answer these questions.**

a Where did the crime in the newspaper headline take place?
b How old is the average burglar in Britain?
c Who does Olive Mattocks blame for the trouble?
d What would reduce crime, according to PC Robinson?
e What does Rose Leach say about young people today?
f What does Harry Richards blame for the amount of crime in his area?

a crime an act which is against the law

car theft stealing cars or stealing objects from cars

a break-in when a building is entered by force and things are stolen

youth crime crime committed by young people

a burglar someone who breaks into a building and steals things

low moral standards poor standards or behaviour, a lack of principles

mugging when a person is attacked in the street and their money or valuables are stolen

Key language

Look at these sentences.

If people had more things to do, there would be less crime in our town.
If young people had more respect, there wouldn't be so much crime.

if + subject + simple past verb + object, subject + *would(n't)* + object
(imaginary situation) (possible result)

These are examples of second conditional sentences. (Compare with zero conditional, page 7 and first conditional, page 63.) We use them to talk about 'unreal' or imaginary situations and their possible results. Besides the modal verb *would*, we can also use *might* and *could* to express different degrees of possibility. (See page 27.)

Now turn to page 87 for practice!

Talk about it

4 **Work with a partner. What would reduce youth crime in your country? Use the stem sentences below to help you.**

- If teenagers didn't ...,
- If there were more ...,
- If communities ...,

There's nothing to do!

5 **Do you agree with the statements below? Share your opinions with a partner.**

- Teenagers today are spoilt. They have more advantages than their parents had.
- Parents should be responsible for their children's actions.
- Young people turn to crime because they are bored.
- Teenagers today do not know the difference between right or wrong.

Write about it

6 **If you could improve the facilities for young people in your town, what would you do? Write about your ideas. Begin like this:**

If I could improve the facilities for young people in my town, the first thing I would do is ...
Then, I would ...
I would also ...

Joyriding may look like fun, but it's dangerous and it's against the law.

Tune in

1 **Before you listen. Have you ever seen a crime? Has anyone ever stolen something from you?**

2 **Listen to Gemma, 16 describing how she got into trouble with the police. Tick (✓) the crimes below that you hear mentioned. Check any words you do not know in the *Word list*.**

☐ burglary	☐ mugging	☐ shoplifting
☐ joyriding	☐ assault	☐ car theft

3 **Listen to the recording again and put the events below in the correct order. The first one has been done for you.**

a Gemma and Darren were arrested. ☐
b Gemma and her friends started shoplifting. ☐
c A woman called the police. ☐
d Gemma and Darren stole a car. ☐
e Gemma and Darren hit another car. ☐
f Gemma started bunking off school. 1

bunking off *(slang)* going absent from school without permission
shoplifting stealing things from shops
joyriding *(slang)* stealing a car and driving it dangerously for fun
to chase to follow someone at speed
terrifying very frightening
arrested stopped by the police and taken to the police station
a final warning an official warning from the police

Key language

Look at these sentences.

I thought he was the coolest boy ever.
We took the things that were easiest to steal.
The most terrifying experience of my life.
That time the worst didn't happen.

These sentences contain the superlative form of an adjective. (Compare with comparatives on page 65.)
We use superlatives when we want to compare a person or thing to all the others in its group: *the coolest boy ever.*

To form the superlative of adjectives which take *'er'* or *'ier'* in their comparative form, we add *the* and *'est'* or *'iest'*: *the coolest, the easiest*.
Those adjectives which take *more* in their comparative form, have *the most* as their superlative: *the most terrifying*.
There are some irregular superlatives: *bad, worse, the worst; good, better, the best; far, further, the furthest*

Now turn to page 87 for practice!

Sounds like this!

4 **Look at the adjectives below. Put each in the correct column according to its superlative form as in the example.**

angry, stupid, cool, easy, bad, good, difficult, sad, happy, dangerous

1	2	3	4
'est'	*'iest'*	*the most*	*irregular*
stupidest			

Now listen and check your answers.

"I passed! This is the happiest day of my life!"

Talk about it

5 **Read the questions below, then write three more of your own. Work in pairs and ask each other the questions.**

- When was the happiest day of your life?
- When was the worst day of your life?
- What is the most difficult thing you have ever done?
- ....?
- ....?
- ....?

6 **Work in groups of three or four people and discuss the questions below.**

- Who was responsible for Gemma's problems; her parents, her school, Darren, or Gemma herself?
- Do you feel sorry for Gemma?
- Why do teenagers bunk off school?
- Is teenage crime a problem in your country?

Mind maps

That's cool!

1 **Mind maps are a good way to remember new words. Here is a mind map for *That's cool!,* (page 6). Look at it carefully to see how it works. Then, put the following words and phrases into the correct spaces (i-iii) on the mind map.**

- fashion
- don't wear a baseball cap
- Wicked!

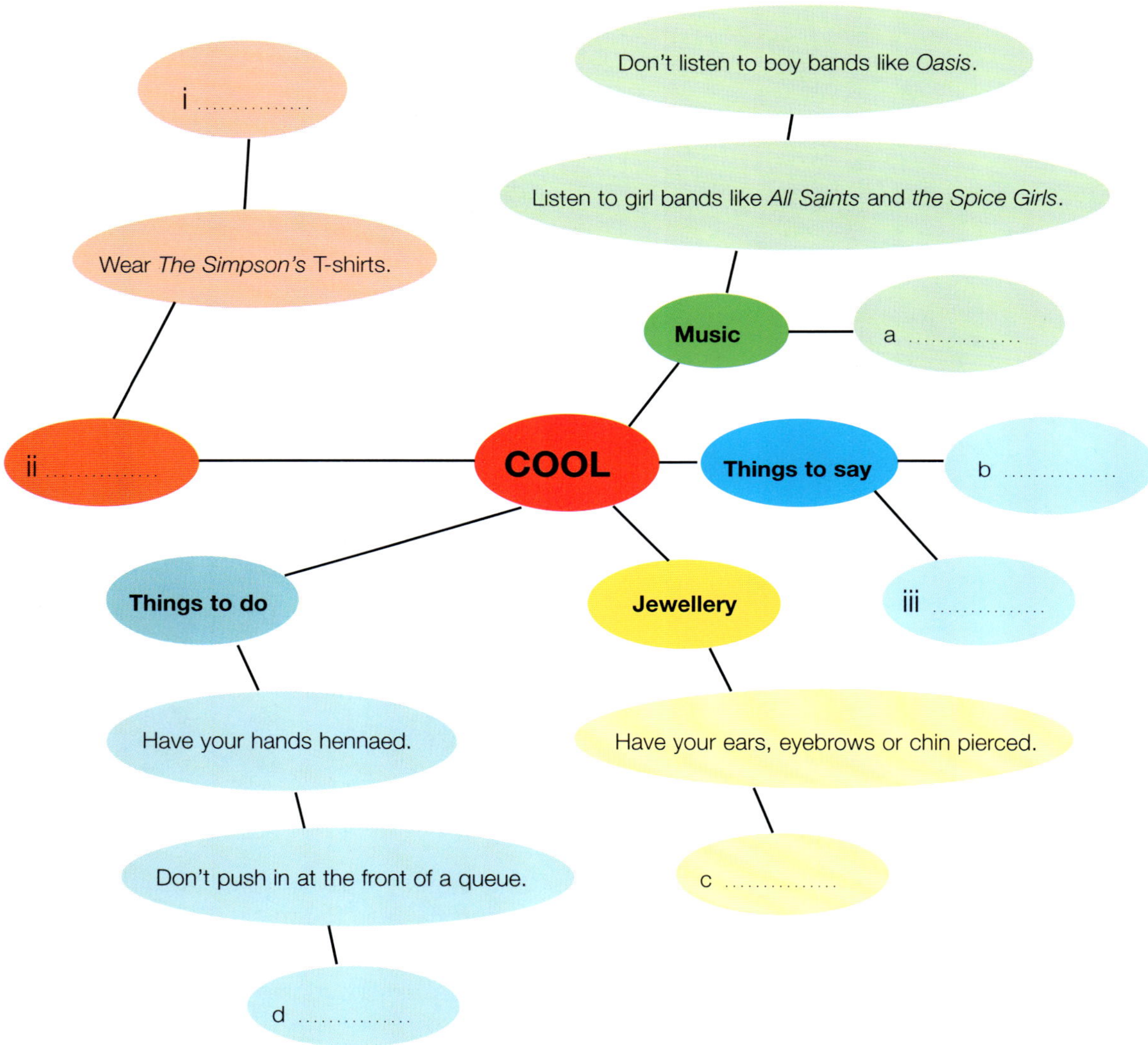

2 **When you have you have completed the *Talk about it* activity on page 7, fill in bubbles (a-d) with your own cool ideas for music, things to say, jewellery and things to do.**

Let's see a movie

1 Look at this mind map for *Let's see a movie*, page 36. Fill in the subject at the centre (i), and then complete the mind map.

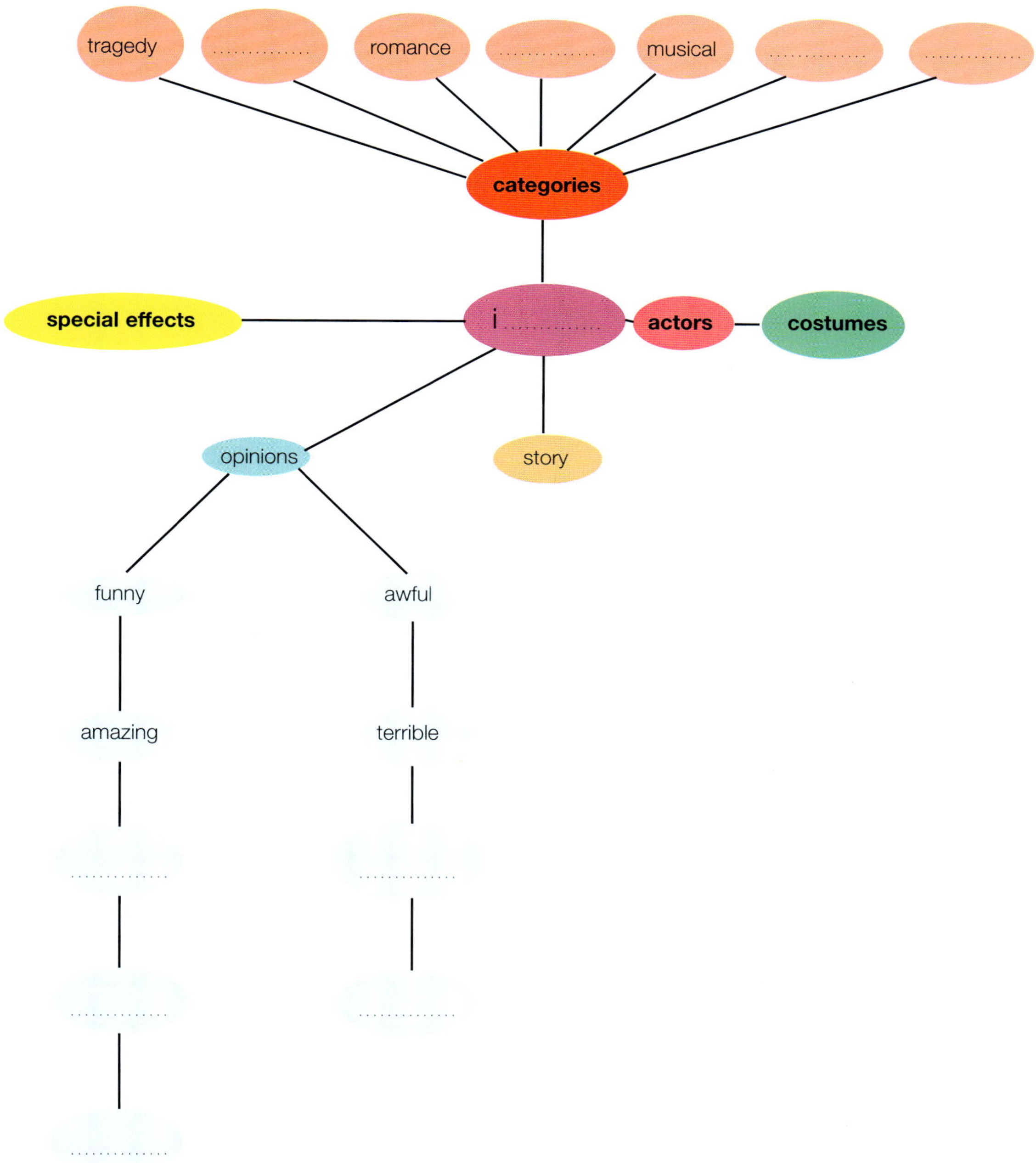

That's cool!

Key language Page 7

1 **Match the two halves (a-g and i-vii) to make zero conditional sentences.**

a If you push in at the front of a queue, *people get annoyed.* ....

b If you want to shock your parents, ...

c If you want to sound cool, ...

d Listen to girl bands, ...

e If you want to do the latest thing, ...

f Don't wear a baseball cap, ...

g Wear Adidas or Nike trainers, ...

i say "Wicked!"
ii if you want to be 'in'.
iii people get annoyed.
iv get your ears or eyebrows pierced.
v if you want to look trendy.
vi have your hands hennaed.
vii if you want to wear the right shoes.

2 **Complete these sentences. Then, compare your answers with a partner.**

a If I want to look cool, I wear ....

b I ...., if I want to decorate my body.

c If I want to listen to some cool music, I ....

d I never ...., if I want to look cool.

e If I want to go to a trendy place with my friends, I ....

f My friends and I ...., if the weather's bad at weekends.

Key language Page 8

3 **Make questions using the jumbled words below, as in the example.**

a name 's your what?
What's your name? ....

b to school do go which you?
....

c you from where are?
....

d easily make you friends do?
....

e buy do clothes your you where?
....

f music do like kind what of you?
....

g sisters any have brothers or you got?
....

4 **Read the dialogue below carefully and write the questions.**

Anita Hello. ....?
Dave My name's David. Dave for short.
Anita 'Nice to meet you, Dave. My name's Anita. ....?
Dave I'm sixteen.
Anita Where are you from?
Dave Bristol, it's a city in England. And you?
Anita I'm from Bonn, in Germany. ....?
Dave Yes, I've got a sister. She's eighteen. What about you?
Anita I've got a brother. He's twelve.
Dave ....?
Anita Me? Oh, I really like *Boyzone* and Céline Dion. And you?
Dave I really like *All Saints*. I must go now. 'Nice talking to you!
Anita See you around! Bye!

Girl power

Vocabulary Page 12

1 **Read the definitions and write the school subject, as in the example.**

a In this subject, you study the past. *History*

b You learn about other countries during these lessons. G ....

c This subject looks at living things, such as people, animals and plants. B ....

d We study the lives of famous artists and learn how to paint and draw. A ....

e This is the language that is spoken in France. We study it twice a week! F ....

f This subject is the science of numbers. M ....

g In this subject, you learn to play an instrument, such as the violin or the flute. M ....

Key language Page 11

2 **Make sentences in the present continuous, using the words below. The first one has been done for you.**

a Who/play/the piano?
Who is playing the piano?

b I/eat/an apple.
....

c People/dance/in the street.
....

d The family/watch/a video.
....

e We/buy/a new car.
....

f What/your brother/doing?
....

g Who/make/that noise?
....

3 **Work with a partner. Look around your classroom and say what is happening. Begin like this:**

A The teacher is ...

B Yes! Look at *(name)*! He/She's ...

Key language Page 12

4 **Write questions to ask another student about the things he/she has got at home. Use the list below to help you, then add two more things of your own.**

- a computer
- a CD player
- a video recorder
- ....
- ....

Begin like this:

A Have you got a computer at home?

B Yes, we have./No, we haven't.

5 **Gary and Steve are talking about their schools. Read the conversation and fill in the gaps with *has*, *'s*, *have*, *'ve* and *got*, as in the example.**

Steve My school *has got* about 2,000 students.

Gary Really? We .... about 1,000 students, I think.

Steve Is your school for boys only?

Gary No, we .... girls at our school, too! It's great!

Steve We .... really good sports facilities at our school.

.... you .... a swimming pool at your school?

Gary Yes, we .... We .... everything!

Our school .... even .... squash courts!

Shopping

Vocabulary **Pages 14–16**

1 The words in this quiz are on pages 14 and 16. Read the definitions and un-jumble the letters to form the correct word.

a an activity you do when you are free AMPSIET *pastime*

b a time when the shops reduce their prices HET LESSA ....

c something which is for sale at a very good price RNAIGBA ....

d the place in a shop where you can try clothes on NGHNAGCI ROMO ....

e the price of something is less than before DCERUDE ....

f money, notes and coins SAHC ....

g someone who loves shopping and can't stop POSOCHAHLI ....

Key language **Page 15**

2 Look at the activities below and write about how you feel about doing each of them. Use *love*, *like*, *enjoy*, *don't mind*, *don't like* and *hate*.

a visit/shopping malls
I hate visiting shopping malls.

b travel/by train
....

c do/homework
....

d tidy/my bedroom
....

e queue/in shops
....

f buy/presents
....

g go/to supermarkets ....

3 Complete these sentences. Then, compare your sentences with a partner.

a I love ....

b I really enjoy ....

c I don't mind ....

d I really don't like ....

e I absolutely hate ....

Key language **Page 17**

4 Put the words in the correct order to make a sentence, as in the example.

a won't cash it for I pay in
I won't pay for it in cash.

b larger ask I'll have they a if in it size
....

c I think I'll shopping tomorrow go
....

d the credit I'll card for shoes by pay
....

e these ask have they jeans if in I'll black
....

f I buy won't sales the this wait today, I'll T-shirt for ....

5 You are visiting your boy/girlfriend. Write a reply to each of his/her comments, as in the example.

Friend I need a cup of coffee!
You *OK! I'll make it for you!*

Friend There's someone knocking at the door!
You *OK!* ....

Friend I would love the new *All Saints'* CD!
You *Fine!* ....

Friend I'm hungry!
You *No problem!* ....

Friend I haven't got any money.
You *That's OK.* ....

Friend This flat is so untidy!
You *Yes, but don't worry.* ....

Be a designer!

Vocabulary — Pages 18–20

1 The words in this quiz are on pages 18 and 20. Read the clues and write the word(s) in the spaces.

a elegant and refined *sophisticated*
b decorations made by sewing e..................
c difficult or testing t..................
d cotton and silk, for example t..................
e the shape or form of something t..................
f Valentino and Versace, for example d..................
g they are used to close shirts and coats b..................
h position, job r..................
i unconventional and bizarre o..................
j strange, unexpected w..................
k the course you do at university d..................
l an important women's fashion magazine V..................

Key language — Page 19

2 Complete these sentences about Stella McCartney by putting the correct verb in the simple past. Then put the sentences in order.

a She *design/work/show* for the British designer Betty Jackson. ☐
b She *work/notice/study* for a tailor in Savile Row. ☐
c Stella *notice/get/employ* a job with Christian Lacroix. ☐
d She *study/do/want* A levels and then took a year off before university. ☐
e Chloé *employ/work/interview* Stella as a fashion designer. ☐
f She *study/do/show* for a degree in fashion design. ☐

3 Put the following regular simple past verbs in the correct column according to how the '*ed*' ending is pronounced: /t/, /d/ or /ɪd/.

enjoyed wanted studied noticed watched employed showed finished pronounced

/t/	/d/	/ɪd/
noticed		

Key language — Page 20

4 Complete this table of irregular verbs, as in the example.

infinitive	simple past
be	*was/were*
....	saw
choose	....
....	got
make	....
spend	....
....	became
go	....
....	put
do	....

5 Complete these simple past sentences, as in the example.

a Sandy *Did* you *see* the X Files on TV last night?
Jane Yes, I did. It .... very scary!

b Martin What .... you do yesterday?
Liz I .... the whole day working on my History project.

c Mum Which jeans .... you choose to wear to the party?
Son I .... the Levis, they are my favourites.

d Robin .... you go out last night?
Jo No, I .... We stayed in and .... a video.

e Police officer Where .... you last Saturday night?
Man I .... at the disco with my friends.

f Vito What .... you .... for dinner last night?
Gino I .... spaghetti bolognese, your favourite!

g Richard Where .... you put my glasses, I can't find them!
Betty I .... them on the table. Look!

Don't be cruel

Vocabulary — Page 24

1 Look in the grid below and find the names of six animals. Complete each sentence below with the name of one of the animals.

P	O	T	B	E	L	L	I	E	D	P	I	G	S
X	T	A	R	A	N	T	U	L	A	S	M	V	N
T	Y	R	U	C	X	D	A	S	W	Z	A	A	A
D	F	G	H	O	R	S	E	S	V	G	J	Z	K
I	G	U	A	N	A	S	Z	B	N	M	J	E	E
K	I	T	T	E	N	S	C	V	B	N	Y	U	S

a .... seem dangerous, but they are not.

b .... look scary, but they are gentle.

c .... are fashionable at the moment.

d .... are cute and playful.

e .... are nervous, loyal and gentle.

f .... are ugly, but friendly.

Key language — Page 23

2 Join the two parts (a-g and i-vii), to form sentences about pet care. The first one has been done for you.

a You mustn't *be cruel to your pet*..........

b You must give a rabbit ....

c Hamsters don't need ....

d You must give a horse ....

e You mustn't leave ....

f A dog must have ....

g Mice don't need ....

i a lot of company.

ii a lot of exercise.

iii your pet alone when you go on holiday.

iv a cage to live in.

v be cruel to your pet.

vi a walk every day.

vii meat in their diet.

3 Work in pairs. Imagine you are explaining to visiting aliens from the planet Eptron, what humans need to live. Complete the sentences below, as in the example.

a Humans need *to eat every day*..............

b They need ....

c Humans need to sleep ....

d Humans need to live ....

e They must eat ....

f They mustn't have ....

g Humans need a lot of ....

Key language — Page 24

4 Fill in the gaps below to make adjectives which you can use to describe pets, as in the example.

a F *A* SH *I* *O* N *A* B L E

b N _ R V _ _ S

c L _ Y _ L

d C _ D D L _

e N _ _ S _

f Q _ _ _ T

g P L _ Y F _ _

5 Look again at the adjectives on page 24. Work in groups of three or four. Student A chooses an animal and writes down an adjective from the list to describe it.
For example: dog - *loyal*
Student A calls out the animal's name. The others write down an adjective from the list. If it is the same adjective as Student A's, then you score a point.

Food or poison?

Vocabulary Page 26–28

1 **All the words in this quiz are on pages 26 and 28. Read the clues below and complete the crossword.**

a to stop a disease and make the patient better
b another word for *modify*
c a reaction to something your body does not like
d an organism that causes a disease
e a nasty feeling you get if part of your body is hurt
f a food which is made out of milk
g the soft part of your mouth which you use to talk
h every living thing has these, they decide our characteristics
i if your body does not like something, you are .... to it
j to change something so that it is better
k you grow plants in this
l another word for *make*
m to change slightly, so that the characteristics are different
n a way to introduce a drug into the body
o when part of your body gets bigger, it …

a	c _ _ _
b	_ h _ _ _ _
c	a _ _ _ _ _ _
d	_ _ r _ _
e	_ a _ _
f	c _ _ _ _ _
g	t _ _ _ _ _
h	_ e _ _ _
i	_ _ _ _ r _ _ _
j	i _ _ _ _ _ _
k	s _ _ _
l	_ _ _ _ t _
m	_ _ _ i _ _
n	_ _ _ _ c _ _ _ _
o	s _ _ _ _ _

Key language Page 27

2 **Complete these sentences with *will*, *won't*, *could*, *might* or their negative forms.**

a There .... be problems with genetically modified food.
b Scientists .... create new diseases by mistake.
c Genetically modified plants .... grow bigger and stronger.
d Scientists .... solve the world's food shortage.
e Food .... be cheaper in the future.
f In the future, all crops, such as soya and wheat .... be modified.
g People .... protest about genetically modified food.

Key language Page 29

3 **Two friends are talking about where to eat out. Put their conversation in the correct order. The first one has been done for you.**

Helen	No thanks. I'm not keen on pizzas.	☐
Helen	No thanks. I don't like the food at the snack bar. Let's go to the Chinese restaurant!	☐
Kate	Where shall we go this evening? Would you like to go to the pizzeria?	1
Kate	Yes! Great idea. I'll phone and book a table.	☐
Kate	Oh, OK. Well, how about going to the snack bar, instead?	☐

4 **Work with a partner. One person is A the other is B. Read the instructions below and prepare your part.**

A You want to go to a pop concert on Saturday night. Invite your friend.
B You don't want to go to the pop concert. You hate the noise! Make another suggestion.
C You don't like B's idea. Suggest something else.
B A's suggestion sounds fun. Accept and arrange a time and place to meet.

When you are ready, practice your dialogue.

Born free?

Key language — Page 31

1 **Imagine you are in the *Rainforest Cafe* with a friend. Complete the conversation below, as in the example.**

Waiter — Are you ready to order?

You — Yes. ...I'd... like a *Volcanic Cobb Salad*, please.

Waiter — And you?

Friend — Oh, ... I .... a *Gorilla Cheese Sandwich*, please?

Waiter — .... like anything else?

You — Yes, please. .... I .... a *Maui Chicken Club*, please?

Friend — And I .... like a *Garden of Eden* to start with, please.

Waiter — Thank you. Do .... a drink?

You — Yes, I .... a Coca Cola, and my friend .... a Fanta. Thank you.

2 **Imagine you are giving a special dinner for your friends. Write about the dishes you would prepare and how you would make the evening special.**

Use the example below as a model.

I would begin my special dinner with ...
It is a speciality of my country and it is very tasty. It is made with ... and ...

For the main course, I would serve ...

I would give my friends ... for dessert.
It is quite/easy difficult to make and you need ... and ...

To make the evening special I would ...

Key language — Page 32

3 **Read the dialogue carefully. Then fill in the gaps.**

Mary — Do .... we should still have zoos, Pete?

Pete — Well, personally I .... think they are very good for the animals. The cages are often too small and the animals look bored.

Mary — I .... you. The animals don't have much to do and some look very sad.

Sally — In .... all zoos should be closed. I don't think they are useful for animal study.

Sean — I .... with all of you! Some zoos have breeding programmes and help to reintroduce animals into the wild. If .... zoos have a role to play in conservation today!

Tom — I .... you, Sean. San Diego Zoo in California reintroduced the Arabian White Oryx into Oman. It was extinct there, now the country has a thriving population.

In .... zoos are useful!

4 **Work in groups of four. Look at the statements below about circuses. Read out each and discuss whether you agree or disagree.**

- circuses are cruel
- circus animals are forced to do tricks
- circuses are fun for all the family
- circuses are just for making money
- circus animals do not mind living in cages
- circuses are an important tradition which we should keep

Begin like this:

A Circuses are cruel. What do you think (*B*)?

B Well, in my view ... What's your opinion (*C*)?

C Personally, I think ...

Let's see a movie

Key language Pages 34–35

1 Read the text on page 34 again and decide whether these statements are true or false. Correct the false ones, as in the example.

a The *Titanic* was sailing from Liverpool to New York. F
The Titanic was sailing from Southampton to New York.

b It was the *Titanic*'s second voyage. ☐
....

c The ship's wireless operator was working alone, when he received a warning from the *Carpathia*. ☐
....

d The lookouts were keeping watch, but they weren't using binoculars. ☐
....

e The *Titanic* was sailing too fast towards the iceberg. ☐
....

f None of the passengers were sleeping when the ship hit the iceberg. ☐
....

g The Quartermaster was inspecting the boiler room when he saw water pouring through a gash in the hull. ☐
....

2 Read the text about the *Titanic* again and make notes on the most important points. Then prepare to tell the story to your partner. When you are both ready:

Student A re-tells the story of the *Titanic*. B listens and adds any details A has left out.

Begin like this:

A Well, it was the 12th April 1912 and the *Titanic* was sailing to New York.

B Yes, it was her maiden voyage.

A Right. Bruce Ismay was …

Vocabulary Page 36

3 Fill in the missing letters to give a type of film. Check your answers on page 36.

i H O R R O R
ii … USI … A …
iii TH … I … … E …
iv C … R … O O …
v … O M E … …
vi … C I … N … … F … C T … O …
vii … O M … N C …
viii C … S T … … E D … A … A

Key Language Page 36

4 Dan and Zoe are talking about films. Read their conversation and then fill in the gaps.

Dan Tell me about your favourite film, Zoe.

Zoe Well, I think my favourite must be *Romeo and Juliet*. I saw it last summer.
It was about a young man and woman who met and fell in love.
The tragedy of the story was that their two families hated each other.

Dan Who .... the main actors?

Zoe Leonardo diCaprio and Clare Danes.

Dan What was the acting like?

Zoe It .... brilliant and the costumes .... amazing.

Dan Hmm. I'm not really .... romance. I .... action films ...., like *Terminator*, with Arnold Schwarzenegger.

Zoe Ugh! I don't like action films ....
I like romance films ....

Sport and money

Vocabulary Pages 38–41

1 **Complete the verb table below. Look up any verbs you do not know in the *verb table* on page 96.**

infinitive	simple past	past participle
find	found	found ....
....	met	met
learn	....	....
lose	....	....
....	....	bought
....	won	....
take	....	....
see	saw	....
be	......./.......	....
....	paid	....
become	became	....
break	....	....

Key language Page 39

2 **Put the words in each list in the correct order to make a sentence.**

a has of lot money earned he a
He has earned a lot of money.

b competitions won she has many
....

c become they famous have very
....

d million the paid a have dollars sponsors
....

e he promoted products has many sports
....

f improve taken drugs to their they performance have
....

g an she important has race lost
....

Key language Page 40

3 **Complete these sentences with *ever* and *never*.**

a I have never been to Paris.

b Have you .... met a famous sports star?

c The team have .... won a game.

d Has that athlete .... taken drugs?

e Have they .... promoted a product?

f We've .... seen a major competition.

g She has .... won the World Championship.

4 **Complete the following sentences with a verb from activity 1. Then answer the questions.**

a Have you ever seen the Taj Mahal?
No, I haven't.

b Have you ever .... to Rome?
....

c Have you ever .... something valuable?
....

d Have you ever .... a prize?
....

e Have you ever .... a bone?
....

f Have you ever .... something without paying for it?
....

g Have you ever .... in trouble with the police?
....

Get connected!

Vocabulary — Page 42

1 **Read the definitions and find the correct word or words in the box. The word(s) may be written horizontally, vertically or diagonally.**

a 01273 547834 is my phone _ _ _ _ _ _
b a phone you can carry around with you
c to arrive at a bus stop after the bus has left
d to change your opinion about something
e an expression to use when you are grateful or relieved about something
f to collect someone
g something annoying or something that makes you angry is _ _ _ _ _ _ _ _ _ _ _ _
h to disallow or forbid an activity
i a place where you can always find a phone
j if someone rings you, they _ _ _ _ you

a	c	h	a	n	g	e	y	o	u	r	m
x	m	t	p	**n**	**u**	**m**	**b**	**e**	**r**	d	i
p	i	o	e	i	c	o	m	e	m	i	n
y	s	u	b	d	c	p	l	g	g	r	d
o	s	v	a	i	a	k	j	t	o	r	a
o	t	o	n	u	l	x	u	f	t	i	f
t	h	s	n	p	u	e	i	p	d	t	c
h	e	i	r	q	s	m	p	k	a	a	k
a	b	p	c	a	l	l	u	h	j	t	v
n	u	h	o	v	a	w	b	z	o	i	l
k	s	p	h	o	n	e	b	o	x	n	o
g	o	o	d	n	e	s	s	o	i	g	e

Key language — Page 43

2 **Decide whether the tense in each sentence is simple past, or present perfect. Write *SP*, for simple past and *PP* for present perfect.**

a I bought a mobile phone last year. SP
b Some restaurants have banned mobile phones.
c Since 1985, ten million people have bought mobile phones in Britain.
d I've changed my mind now.
e The first mobile phones appeared in 1985.
f The other night, I missed the bus home.

3 **Match each question (a-f) with the correct answer (i-vi).**

a Where did you go last year?
b Did you buy a mobile phone last Saturday?
c What did you do last New Year?
d Have you decided where to go this evening?
e Has he eaten his breakfast?
f Is your name Giovanni?

i No, I haven't.
ii Yes, he has.
iii We went to Florida.
iv No, it isn't.
v Yes, I did.
vi I had a party.

Key language — Page 44

4 **Read the jumbled telephone conversation below and put it in the correct order.**

Sue	OK, Stefano, I'll give him the message.	
Sue	I'm afraid he's not here at the moment.	
Stefano	Thanks very much. 'Bye.	
Sue	Sure!	
Stefano	Can you tell him Stefano called?	
Sue	Hello, 98704.	1
Stefano	Hello. Is Nick there, please?	
Sue	'Bye.	
Stefano	Can I leave a message?	

5 **Work in pairs. Choose a role card and prepare your part.**

Parent
You are in the bath when Karen, your daughter, phones, (she is at a party). You are not keen to go out and pick her up. Suggest she gets a taxi or goes home from the party with a friend.

Karen
You are at a friend's party and it is late. You have missed the last bus, phone home and ask your parent to pick you up.

When you are both ready, begin like this:

Parent Hello, 893784
karen Hello, Mum/Dad. It's Karen. Listen …

Dear Tracey ...

Vocabulary — Page 46

1 **Read the definitions of these words from page 46, and find the correct word (or words) in the box. They may be written horizontally, vertically or diagonally.**

a something that worries you
b difficult
c sad, miserable
d the legal ending of a marriage
e unhappy or worried
f to stop doing an activity (2 words)
g problems or troubles
h something you give a friend with a problem
i another word for boy or man
j to leave home (permanently) without saying where you are going (2 words)
k to discover (2 words)
l school work

d	i	e	t	x	l	o	p	i	e	s	d
z	e	u	o	l	h	a	r	d	f	d	i
s	r	p	t	i	q	n	o	v	i	b	v
t	e	s	r	s	w	k	b	g	n	i	o
u	a	e	i	e	t	d	l	u	d	e	r
d	r	t	c	b	s	a	e	y	o	v	c
i	j	o	k	e	o	s	m	k	u	k	e
e	a	q	y	e	p	h	e	h	t	o	b
s	a	g	o	n	i	e	s	d	n	m	x
m	e	v	c	g	i	v	e	u	p	s	m
t	d	k	l	u	r	u	n	a	w	a	y
a	d	v	i	c	e	t	o	o	n	s	d

Key language — Page 47

2 **Complete these sentences with *should* or *shouldn't*, as in the example.**

a You *shouldn't* play with matches.
b He .... do his English homework.
c You .... argue with your parents.
d They .... obey their teachers.
e I .... be honest with my friends.
f You .... tell your parents where you are going when you go out.
g Young people .... mix with people who take drugs.

3 **Your friend is studying English, but is finding it very difficult. Give your friend some advice. Use the phrases below to help you.**

a revise each lesson
You should revise each lesson.

b discuss your problems with the teacher
....

c listen to English on the radio or on cable TV
....

d You should ....

e You should ....

f You should ....

Key language — Page 49

4 **Read the dialogue carefully and then complete the questions.**

Lucas Do you *live at home?*
Amy Yes, I live at home with my parents and brother.
Lucas .... your .... strict?
Amy Well, they are strict about school work.
Lucas .... you .... to have boyfriends?
Amy Yes. But I can only go out at weekends.
Lucas .... do people .... dating in Britain?
Amy Well, usually when they are about 14 years old.
Lucas Oh good! What are you doing tonight?

5 **Work in pairs. Look again at page 48 and prepare a role play between Tomoko, the Japanese student and an interviewer.**

Tomoko
Make notes about yourself, your family and school life.

Interviewer
You are going to interview Tomoko. Prepare questions about her life, her family and school.

When you are ready, begin like this:

Interviewer Well, Tomoko. Where are you from?

Kill or cure?

Key language **Page 51**

1 **Read the following sentences about life 30 years ago and decide whether they are true or false. Correct the false ones.**

When you are ready, compare your answers with a partner.

a Thirty years ago people used to go to the barber if they were ill.

False. People went to the doctor. ....

b People didn't have television - they used to listen to the radio.

....

c There used to be fewer cars on the roads.

....

d Most people used to ride a bike to work.

....

e People used to write a lot of letters, as there were no telephones.

....

f Computers used to be the size of a whole room.

....

g People used to be more friendly.

....

2 **Think back to when you were ten years old. Make notes about your school life, your family, your friends and hobbies. Then, when you are ready, work with a partner and ask each other about your past lives.**

Begin like this:

A Where did you use to go to school?

B Well, I used to go to ... school in ...

A Who used to be your best friend?

B A girl called Sabine. Where did you use to live?

Key language **Page 53**

3 **Match the two halves (a-g) and (i-vii) to make sentences about life in 50 years' time.**

a People will talk to each other

by videophone. ....

b We won't go to the beach any more

....

c We will recycle ....

d People will have robots ....

e We will all take holidays ....

f Man will land a rocket ....

g There won't be any more petrol ....

....

i so cars will all run on solar power.
ii all our rubbish.
iii to do their housework.
iv on the moon.
v by videophone.
vi on the planet Mars.
vii as there will be too much pollution.

4 **Use the prompts below and *will*, *won't*, *could*, *might* and *might not* to make predictions about how life could change during the next 100 years.**

a doctors/find/cure for cancer

Doctor's might not find a cure for cancer.

b the world's population/increase

....

c diseases, such as malaria/disappear

....

d there/another world war

....

e oil reserves/run out

....

f there/less poverty

....

g third world countries/richer

....

Have a nose job

Vocabulary — Page 54

1 All the words in this activity are on page 54. Complete all the words across and discover the hidden words running down the puzzle.

a someone who sings as a job
b another word for 'difficult'
c a type of surgery to improve your looks (2 words)
d 'will not'
e a difficulty
f to achieve your goals
g very famous actors or pop singers
h another word for child
i an operation to improve the shape of your nose
j very big
k a female actor
l imperfections of the body (2 words)

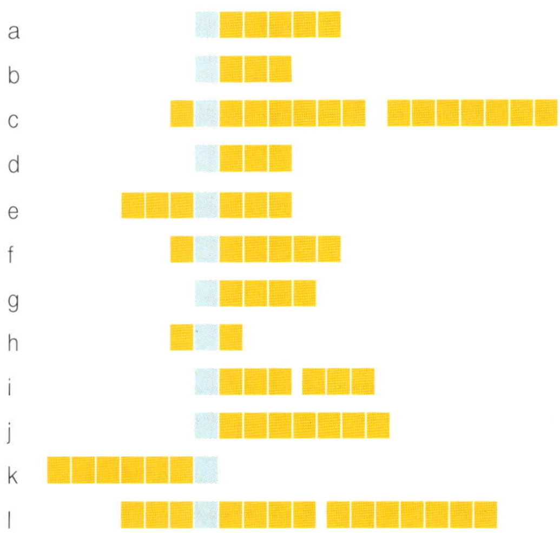

Key language — Page 55

2 Put the words in each list in the correct order to a make sentence. The first one has been done for you.

a going I'm to a nose I'm 16 job have when
I'm going to have a nose job when I'm 16.

b are to nose operate on surgeons going Sammy's? ....

....

c to surf learn this going summer to I'm

....

d you going what tomorrow are do to?

....

e or a going be a she's not dancer to singer

....

f work I'm to at school this hard going year

....

g summer we're next in have a Spain going not to holiday

....

Key language — Page 57

3 Complete the sentences below by putting the adjectives in brackets in the correct order, as in the example.

a He's got ... (*brown/gorgeous/big*) eyes.
He's got gorgeous big brown eyes.

b She's got a ... (*lovely/straight/long*) nose.

....

c She's got ... (*red/curly/beautiful*) hair.

....

d Pigs have got ... (*pale pink/horrible)* eyes.

....

e She's got ... (*brown/short/frizzy)* hair.

....

f He's got ... (*mousy/horrible/long)* hair.

....

g Everyone in the family has got ... (*short/dark/curly)* hair.

....

4 Think of a person in your family, or your best friend and write a description of him or her. Begin like this:

The person I am going to describe is my ...
He/She is ... and ...
He/She has got ... eyes and ... hair.
He/She is ... years old and likes ...

Aliens!

Vocabulary Pages 58–61

1 Read each definition and find the word in the box below. All the hidden words are on pages 58 and 60.

s	x	c	p	e	a	r	t	h
p	c	a	t	i	s	n	r	e
a	d	e	v	n	g	g	a	x
c	a	l	m	d	o	w	n	h
e	r	q	w	k	l	o	s	a
s	s	c	a	r	e	d	l	u
u	f	o	b	g	j	k	a	s
i	e	p	l	a	n	e	t	t
t	k	i	d	n	a	p	o	e
k	i	d	d	i	n	g	r	d

a something you wear when you travel in space
b the name of our planet
c an expression you use when you want someone to be quieter (2 words)
d very tired
e someone who translates
f another word for joking
g frightened, afraid
h to capture someone and hold them against their will
i Mars is an example
j an unidentified flying object

Key language Page 59

2 Change these sentences from active to passive, as in the example.

a The aliens kidnapped me.
I was kidnapped by aliens.
b They took me to their space ship.
....
c They took me into a large blue room.
....
d They told me to sit down.
....
e One of them asked me a lot of questions.
....
f One of them took a sample of my blood.
....
g An alien showed me round their space ship.
....

3 Write the past participle of each of the verbs below. Then, write sentences in the past passive using the verbs and the prompts below.

direct	*directed*	*write*	....
sing	....	*paint*	....
build	....	*produce*	....
compose	....	*invent*	....

a *Titanic*/James Cameron
Titanic was directed by James Cameron
b *Oliver Twist*/Charles Dickens ....
....
c *Waterloo/Abba* ....
....
d The *Mona Lisa*/Leonardo da Vinci ....
e *The Eiffel Tower*/Gustav Eiffel ....
f *Aladdin*/Disney ....
g *1812 overture*/Tchaikovsky ....
h The telephone/Alexander graham Bell
....

Key language Page 61

4 Use the following 'linking words' to complete each sentence. You may use any of them more than once.

when at first meanwhile next then much later finally

a .... I was a child, I lived in France.
b ...., I didn't like him, but .... I knew him better, I liked him very much.
c I was puzzled at first, ... I had a brilliant idea.
d Jim was looking everywhere for Trudy. ...., I was looking for Jim.
e .... that day, Uncle Vincent came to visit.
f ...., I locked the door and went home.
g First put the eggs in a bowl. .... mix the eggs with the butter.

Uniformity?

Vocabulary Page 64

1 **The letters in the words below are in the wrong order. Un-jumble them to make the names of jobs, as in the example.**

a SENUR *nurse*
b EASCHRI ....
c RFEI FRTHGIE ....
d OESLRDI ....
e TLOIP ....
f NKBA KERCL ....
g CELPIO FFCREOI ....
h CISTEUYR UGDAR ....

Key language Page 63

2 **Match the two halves (a-g) and (i-vii) to make first conditional sentences. The first one has been done for you.**

a If my friend is late, I'll
phone her to see what has happened.
b If I lose my train ticket, I'll
....
c If he misses the last bus, he'll
....
d If I see a nice coat in the sales, I'll
....
e If she feels ill tomorrow, she'll
....
f If it's sunny today, we'll
....
g If he does well in the English test, his
....

i walk home or get a taxi.
ii go for a picnic on the beach.
iii buy it.
iv stay in bed and call the doctor.
v Dad will give him £20.00.
vi try to get on the train without buying another one.
vii phone her to see what's happened.

3 **Look at the table below and begin five *if* sentences using one word from each column in your note book. Then, give your sentences to a partner, who must finish them.**
For example: *If my Mum misses the bus,* my dad will have to pick her up.

		Mum	miss	the	bus
		sister	lose	his	keys
If	my	brother	forget	her	money
		aunt	feel		passport
	I	Dad	get	better	ticket
		find	remember		homework
		—	—	my	birthday

Key language Page 65

4 **Complete each sentence with a comparative, as in the example.**

a John looked happy yesterday, but he looks *happier* today.
b The blue blazer is smart, but I think the grey one is ....
c The Japanese restaurant is expensive, but I think the Thai one is ....
d The chocolate cake tastes good, but I think the fruit cake tastes ....
e Our garden is nice, but the garden next door is ....
f My Maths is bad, but my sister's is ....
g Holidays in Spain are cheap, but holidays to Romania are .... at the moment.

5 **Work in pairs and discuss how you would like to improve the following things:**

- your bedroom
- your brothers and sisters
- your teacher
- your clothes
- your boyfriend/girlfriend
- other things

Begin like this:

A Well, to begin with, I'd like a bigger bedroom with ...

In trouble

Vocabulary **Page 69–69**

1 **All the words in this quiz are on pages 66 and 68. Read each definition and complete the crossword. What are the hidden words in the puzzle?**

a stealing a car and driving it dangerously for fun
b youth crime is a .... in Britain
c someone who steals things from people's houses
d stopped by the police and taken to the police station
e to follow someone at speed
f the crime of stealing cars (2 words)
g having a lack of principles (3 words)
h taking things from shops without paying
i attacking someone in the street to steal their money or valuables
j when a building is entered by force (2 words)

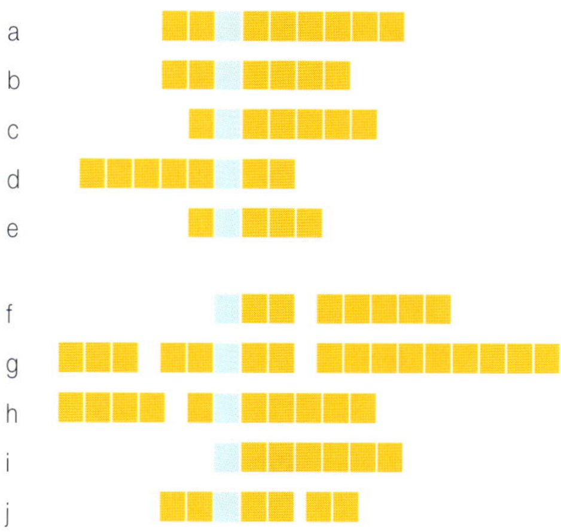

Key language **Page 67**

2 **Complete the following sentences in your own words, as in the example.**

a If teachers were all under 25 years old, *school would be more fun.*

b If animals could talk, ...

c If everyone stopped throwing rubbish on the ground, ...

d If people were kinder to each other, ...

e There would be less youth crime, if ....

Key language **Page 69**

3 **Joe and Lucy are talking about school. Read their conversation and put the dialogue in the correct order. The first one has been done for you.**

Joe	Miss Ludlow is not the best teacher - she's just given me detention!	☐
Lucy	So, which subject do you find the easiest?	☐
Joe	Yes, that's true, but he's the best teacher there is.	☐
Joe	Miss Brown is definitely the coolest teacher.	☐
Lucy	Really? I find English the easiest. Who is the coolest teacher?	1
Joe	Well, I find Maths the easiest and English the most difficult.	☐
Lucy	Yes, she is. And Mr Harvey is definitely the most frightening.	☐
Lucy	No, I think the best teacher in the school is Miss Ludlow.	☐

4 **Work in groups of three or four. One person in each group chooses a category from the list below. The other members of the group must give an example. If you can't think of one, you are out of the game.**

- the coolest pop stars
- the best thing you've ever eaten
- the worst thing you've ever eaten
- the biggest mistake you have ever made
- the easiest school subject
- the most difficult school subject

For example:

A The coolest pop stars!
B Madonna!
C *Boyzone*!
D I can't think!
A Sorry! You're out!

Key

(adj)	=	adjective
(adv	=	adverb
(adv phr)	=	adverbial phrases
(ce)	=	common expression
(coll)	=	colloquial
(det)	=	determiner
(infml)	=	informal
(n)	=	noun
(np)	=	noun phrase
(pv)	=	phrasal verb
(sl)	=	slang
(v)	=	verb
(vp)	=	verb phrase

A

act (something) out (v) *17* /ækt'aʊt/ take a part in a dialogue, act a part

action (adj) *36* /'ækʃən/ a film where there is a lot of fighting, movement, excitement

adrenalin (n) *28* /ə'drenəlɪn/ a chemical produced by your body to make your heart beat faster

advances (n) *50* /əd'vɑ:nsɪz/ developments, improvements, changes that bring progress

affirmative (adj) *51* /ə'fɜ:mətɪv/ say 'yes'

ahead (adv) *34* /ə'hed/ in front of something

allow (v) *43* /ə'laʊ/ to permit, to let something happen

amateur (n) *38* /'æmətə/ a person who takes part in a sport for which they are not paid, not a professional

ambitions (n) *20* /æm'bɪʃənz/ the things someone wants to do to become successful, rich, powerful

ambitious (adj) *10* /æm'bɪʃəz/ determined to be successful, rich, powerful

application (n) *18* /æplɪ'keɪʃən/ a formal written request for a job or place at a college or university

argue (v) *46* /'ɑ:gju:/ to disagree with someone, usually in an angry way

assault (n) *68* /ə'sɔ:lt/ the crime of attacking someone

athletics (n) *38* /æθ'letɪks/ sports such as running and jumping

attitude (n) *14* /'ætɪtju:d/ idea, state of mind, way of thinking

attractive (adj) *54* /ə'træktɪv/ nice to look at

audience (n) *38* /'ɔ:dɪəns/ a group of people who watch others performing

average (adj) *66* /'ævərɪdʒ/ having qualities that are typical, ordinary

awful (adj) *36* /'ɔ:fəl/ very bad

B

ban (v) *22* /bæn/ to stop, to disallow

band (n) *6* /bænd/ group of people playing popular music

bandage (n) *50* /'bændɪdʒ/ a narrow piece of cloth to tie around a part of the body that has been injured

barbaric (adj) *50* /bɑ:'bærɪk/ very cruel, violent

baseball cap (n) *72* /'beɪsbɔ:l kæp/ a type of hat you wear when playing baseball

be associated with (vp) *56* /'æsəʊʃɪəɪtɪd/ connected with, have something to do with

be for (something) (vp) *64* /fɔ:/ to agree with

be forced (to do something) (vp) *78* /fɔ:st/ to be made to do something you do not want to do

be into (something) (vp) *6* /'ɪntu:/ to be very interested in, keen on something

be keen on (vp) *29* /ki:n/ to like something very much

be proud of (vp) *20* /praʊd/ to feel pleased with one's achievements

(be) to blame (vp) *66* / bleɪm/ to be responsible for something bad

behaviour (n) *32* /bɪ'heɪvjə/ the way an animal or person acts or functions in particular situations

believe (v) *50* /bə'li:v/ to be sure something is true

big business (n) *38* /bɪg' bɪznɪs/ a commercial activity that makes a lot of money

blazer (n) *62* /'bleɪzə/ a jacket, sometimes with the badge of a school on it

blockbuster (n)(infml) *34* /'blɒkbʌstə/ a book or film that is very good or successful

blood (n) *50* /blʌd/ the red liquid that pumps around your body

blouse (n) *62* /blaʊz/ a woman's shirt

bones (n) *52* /bəʊnz/ the hard parts that form the skeleton of a body

book (v) *77* /bʊk/ to reserve a place

boredom (n) *66* /ˈbɔːdəm/ the feeling that there is nothing interesting to do

bowl (n) *85* /bəʊl/ a round, deep dish

branches (n) *30* /ˈbrɑːntʃɪz/ parts of a tree on which leaves grow

break a record (vp) *69* /breɪk ə ˈrekɔːd/ to do something better than any previous time

break in (v) *66* /breɪk ˈɪn/ to enter a building by force

bridge (of a ship) (n) *34* /brɪdʒ/ *(in this context)* part of a ship from which an officer controls it

brilliant (adj) *37* /ˈbrɪljənt/ very good, excellent

bring up (pv) *10* /brɪŋ ʌp/ to educate and care for a child until it is grown up

burglary (n) *68* /ˈbɜːglərɪ/ the crime of getting into a building and stealing things

by mistake (np) *26* /baɪ mɪˈsteɪk/ something done in error, without intending to

C

cage (n) *24* /keɪdʒ/ a place made with wire or bars where animals are kept

captivity (n) *32* /kæpˈtɪvɪtɪ/ the state of being kept in a cage, not allowed to go where you want

car theft (np) *68* /ˈkaː θeft/ the crime of stealing cars

career (n) *18* /kəˈrɪə/ a job or profession that you have been trained for

cartoon (n) *36* /kɑːˈtuːn/ a film made by a series of moving drawings

channel (v) *52* /ˈtʃænl/ to direct towards

chat (v) *8* /tʃæt/ to talk in a friendly, informal way

chess (n) *8* /tʃes/ a game played by two people on a black and white board with shaped wooden pieces

circus (n) *78* /ˈsɜːkəs(ɪz)/ travelling people (and animals) who entertain with clever, dangerous or funny acts

classmates (n) *15* /ˈklaːsmeɪts/ other students in your class

climate (n) *30* /ˈklaɪmət/ weather conditions of a place

collar (n) *23* /ˈkɒlə/ *(in this context)* a piece of leather put around an animal's neck for identification

collection (n) *18* /kəˈlekʃən/ *(in this context)* a number of different pieces of clothing designed by the same person

collision (n) *34* /kəˈlɪʃən/ an accident in which two things hit each other

column (n) *19* /ˈkɒləm/ *(in this context)* a list of words

come second to (vp) *20* /kʌm ˈsekənd tuː/ to be less important than

comedy (n) *36* /ˈkɒmədi/ a funny film/book

common (adj) *26* /ˈkɒmən/ existing in large quantities

company servant (np) *64* /kʌmpənɪ ˈsɜːvənt/ a person who is controlled by the company

competition (n) *18* /kɒmpəˈtɪʃən/ a situation where one person tries to be more successful than another

complain (of something) (v) *50* /kəmˈpleɪn/ *(in this context)* to say that you feel ill

confidence (n) *12* /ˈkɒnfɪdəns/ belief in yourself, feeling that you can do something

contribute (to) (v) *34* /kənˈtrɪbjʊːt/ *(in this context)* to help cause an event

conventional (adj) *52* /kənˈvenʃənəl/ an accepted or usual way of doing something

cope (with) (v) *46* /ˈkəʊp wɪð/ to deal with, to manage successfully

costume drama (np) *36* /ˈkɒstjʊm ˈdrɑːmə/ a historical film with people wearing clothes of that period

couple (n) *48* /ˈkʌpl/ two people who are having a romantic relationship

crooked (adj) *56* /ˈkrʊkɪd/ not straight

crop (n) *27* /krɒp/ a plant that is grown by farmers to be eaten (e.g. wheat, rice.)

cuddly (adj) *24* /ˈkʌdlɪ/ someone or something that makes you feel you want to hold it

cure (v) *50* /kjʊə/ to make someone who is ill, well again

cut (v) *50* /kʌt/ to make an incision using a sharp tool, to make something shorter (e.g. hair)

cute (adj)(infml) *24* /kjuːt/ sweet, attractive, pretty

D

dangerous (adj) *24* /ˈdeɪndʒərəs/ able to hurt you, a situation which involves a lot of risk

decorate (v) *72* /ˈdekəreɪt/ to add ornaments, patterns to make more beautiful

designer clothes (np) *21* /dɪˈzaɪnə kləʊðz/ clothes that are made by a particular, (usually famous) designer

dessert (n) *78* /dɪˈzɜːt/ the sweet dish served at the end of a meal

detention (n) *87* /dɪˈtenʃən/ when you have to stay late at school as a punishment

dialogue (n) *17* /ˈdaɪəlɒg/ conversation between two or more people

diary (n) *59* /ˈdaɪrɪ/ a book in which you write things that happen each day

(a) diet of (np) *24* /ˈdaɪət/ the kind of food someone or something eats

disco (n) *8* /ˈdɪskəʊ/ a club or party where people dance to pop music

disease (n) *50* /dɪˈziːz/ an illness or unhealthy condition

dish (n) *78* /dɪʃ/ *(in this context)* food cooked or prepared in a particular way as part of a meal

don't mind (vp) *14* /dəʊnt ˈmaɪnd/ to feel neutral about something

dream partner (np) *57* /driːm ˈpɑːtnə/ the perfect person to be with (romantically)

drug (n) *38* /drʌg/ *(in this context)* a chemical taken to improve your ability

dull (adj) *36* /dʌl/ not very interesting

E

earn (v) *38* /ɜːn/ to receive money for work

Earth (n) *58* /ɜːθ/ the planet that we live on

Earthling (n) *59* /ˈɜːθlɪŋ/ a science-fiction word to describe someone from the planet Earth

easily (adv) *9* /ˈiːzəlɪ/ without difficulty, without a problem

educational (adj) *32* /edʒuˈkeɪʃnəl/ of or about providing education

embarrassed (adj) *8* /ɪmˈbærəst/ feel awkward, shy, self-conscious

energy (n) *52* /ˈenədʒɪ/ physical or mental strength, effort

entertainment (n) *66* /entəˈteɪnmənt/ things that amuse or interest people

equal (adj) *62* /ˈɪːkwəl/ having the same rights or chances

essential (adj) *43* /ɪˈsenʃəl/ extremely important

evidence (n) 12 /ˈevɪdəns/ facts that make you believe something is true

ex-boyfriend/girlfriend (np)(infml) *45* /eks ˈbɔɪfrend/ˈgɜːlfrend/ former boyfriend/girlfriend

exercise (n) *23* /ˈeksəsaɪz/ physical activity to keep you fit

experience (v) *30* /ɪkˈspɪərɪəns/ to feel something

experience (n) *58* /ɪkˈspɪərɪəns/ something that happens to you

expert (n) *26* /ˈekspɜːt/ a specialist in a subject

expression (n) *31* /ɪkˈspreʃn/ phrase, way of saying something, short sentence

extinct (adj) *78* /ɪkˈstɪŋkt/ an animal or plant that no longer exists

eyebrow (n) *6* /ˈaɪbraʊ/ the line of hair above the eye

F

fabric (n) *18* /ˈfæbrɪk/ material, cloth used to make clothes

facilities (n) *67* /fəˈsɪlɪtɪz/ rooms, equipment or services that are provided for a particular purpose

fair (adj) *57* /feə/ light-coloured hair or skin

fashion accessory (np) *43* /ˈfæʃən əkˈsesərɪ/ something you wear or carry because it is fashionable

fashion house (n) *18* /ˈfæʃən haʊs/ a company that produces a particular brand of clothes (usually expensive)

fashionable (adj) *24* /ˈfæʃnəbəl/ trendy, popular

fight (v) *52* /faɪt/ to try to stop, to combat

flash (v) *58* /flæʃ/ to shine brightly for a short time

forbid (v) *81* /fəˈbɪd/ to disallow, to tell someone they must not do something

friendly (adj) *24* /ˈfrendlɪ/ behaving towards someone in a way that shows you like them

frizzy (adj) *57* /ˈfrɪzɪ/ hair that is tightly curled, wiry

fun (adj) *24* /fʌn/ an experience or thing that is enjoyable, exciting

G

get on with (pv) *48* /get ˈɒn wɪð/ to have a friendly relationship with

go out with (pv) *46* /gəʊ ˈaʊt wɪð/ to date, to have a romantic relationship with

go red (vp) *8* /gəʊ ˈred/ when you feel shy and your face becomes red

grateful (adj) *80* /ˈgreɪtfəl/ thankful, feeling gratitude

grow up (pv) *54* /grəʊ ˈʌp/ to become an adult

gun-thing (n)(infml) *60* /ˈgʌnθɪŋ/ something that looks like a gun

guy (n)(infml) *46* /gaɪ/ man

gym (gymnasium) (n) *12* /dʒɪm/ a hall with equipment for doing physical exercise

H

habits (n) *15* /ˈhæbɪts/ something that you do regularly

hamster (n) *23* /ˈhæmstə/ a small animal, like a mouse, without a tail

hang on (pv) *44* /ˈhæŋ ɑn/ to wait for a short time (usually on the phone)

hang out (pv) *7* /ˈhæŋ aʊt/ to spend time in one place with a group of friends

hang round (pv)(infml) *68* /hæŋ ˈraʊnd/ to wait or stay somewhere with no real purpose

hard (adj) *28* /hɑːd/ *(in this context)* difficult, in a way that is upsetting

have (something) left (vp) *14* /hæv ˈleft/ to have something remaining

(have a) police record (np) *68* /pəliːs ˈrekɔːd/ to be known to the police

healthy (adj) *54* /ˈhelθɪ/ physically well and strong

hennaed (adj) *6* /ˈhenəd/ coloured with a red dye

historical events (np) *35* /hɪsˈtɒrɪkəl ɪˈvents/ things that happened in the past

honest (adj) *46* /ˈɒnɪst/ truthful, not hiding the facts

horror (adj) *36* /ˈhɒrə/ causing fear, disgust, shock

human (n) *59* /ˈhjuːmən/ a man, woman or child

hunt (for) (v) *15* /ˈhʌnt fɔː/ to look/search for

I

I'm afraid (ce) *44* /əˈfreɪd/ used to politely give someone some bad news

iceberg (n) *34* /ˈaɪsbɜːg/ a large mass of ice floating in the sea

in favour of (adj) *63* /ɪn ˈfeɪvə ɑv/ agree with

in progress (np) *35* /ɪn ˈprəʊgres/ taking place, happening

in spite of (adv phr) *54* /ɪn ˈspaɪt ɒv/ not being prevented by something

in which case (det) *46* /ɪn wɪtʃ ˈkeɪs/ used to talk about a situation you have just mentioned

individuals (n) *64* /ɪndɪˈvɪdjəlz/ people considered independently from each other, not as a group

interrogative (adj) *51* /ɪntəˈrɒgətɪv/ a sentence that asks a question, or has the form of a question

interrupt (v) *35* /ɪntəˈrʌpt/ to suddenly stop an action or activity

interview (v) *15* /ˈɪntəvjuː/ to ask questions for a particular reason

invent (v) *42* /ɪnˈvent/ to make something new for the first time ever

investigate (v) *22* /ɪnˈvestɪgeɪt/ to try to find out the truth about something

involve (v) *14* /ɪnˈvɒlv/ include

involved (adj) *22* /ɪnvˈɒlvd/ *(in this context)* the amount of work, money etc. that is needed to succeed

J

jewellery (n) *7* /ˈdʒuːəlrɪ/ rings, necklaces etc.

K

kinds (of) (n) *31* /ˈkaɪnz ɒv/ types of

L

labelling (n) *26* /ˈleɪblɪŋ/ labels put on goods to show the contents

laboratory (n) *12* /ləˈbɒrətrɪ/ the place where people do scientific experiments

land (v) *59* /lænd/ to arrive somewhere by air or boat

later (on) (adv) *16* /leɪtə ˈɑn / at a time in the future

like crazy (ce)(infml) *60* /laɪk ˈkreɪzɪ/ very quickly or very hard

lock (a door) (v) *87* /lɒk/ to close a door securely with a key

logo (n) *38* /ˈləʊgəʊ/ a small design that is the official sign of a company

look cool (vp) *10* /lʊk kuːl/ to be fashionable, trendy, to look attractive

look like (v) *8* /ˈlʊk laɪk/ to be the same as, similar to

loyal (adj) *24* /ˈlɔɪəl/ someone who supports something or someone

lucky (adj) *8* /ˈlʌkɪ/ fortunate to be able to do something

luxury (adj) *34* /ˈlʌkʃərɪ/ expensive, for pleasure or enjoyment

M

machine (n) *51* /məˈʃiːn/ an appliance, a piece of equipment to do a particular job, (e.g. dishwasher)

make money (vp) *32* /meɪk ˈmʌnɪ/ to earn or gain money

malaria (n) *88* /məˈleərɪə/ a tropical disease people get from mosquito bites

massage (n) *52* /ˈmæsɑːʒ/ the action of pressing or rubbing someone's body with your hand

matches (n) *82* /ˈmætʃɪz/ small wooden sticks used to light a fire or cigarette

meanwhile (adv) *61* /ˈmiːnwaɪl/ at the same time that something else is happening

medicine (n) *50* /ˈmedsən/ *(in this context)* the study of illnesses and injuries

mention (v) *66* /ˈmenʃən/ to talk briefly about something in a piece of writing or a conversation

message (n) *34* /ˈmesɪdʒ/ a written (or spoken) piece of information that you send to someone

mix (with) (v) *82* /mɪks/ to socialise with, be friends with

modify (v) *77* /ˈmɒdɪfaɪ/ to change something slightly

mousy (hair) (adj) *56* /ˈmaʊsɪ/ dull brown hair

mugging (n) *68* /mʌgɪŋ/ the crime of attacking and robbing someone in a public place

murder (n) *66* /ˈmɜːdə/ the crime of deliberately killing someone

muscles (n) *52* /ˈmʌsəlz/ the pieces of flesh inside your body that you use to move

musical (n) *36* /ˈmjuːzɪkəl/ a film where the actors sing and dance as part of the drama

My pleasure! (ce) *12* /maɪ ˈpleʒə/ a way to reply when someone has thanked you for something

negative (adj) *51* /ˈnegətɪv/ say 'no'

N

nervous (adj) *8* /ˈnɜːvəs/ not confident, afraid

noisy (adj) *24* /ˈnɔɪzɪ/ making a lot of sound which disturbs other people

nowadays (adv) *10* /ˈnaʊədeɪz/ now, in the present time

O

obey (v) *82* /əʊˈbeɪ/ to do what someone says

odd (adj) *64* /ɒd/ strange, unusual

organism (n) *77* /ɔːgənɪzm/ a living thing

open (adj) *10* /ˈəʊpən/ *(in this context)* approachable, not restricted

opposite sex (np) *11* /ɒpəzɪt ˈseks/ girls (if you're a boy), boys (if you are a girl)

order (v) *31* /ˈɔːdə/ to ask for

outer space (np) *58* /aʊtə ˈspeɪs/ the space outside the Earth's atmosphere

P

panda (n) *32* /ˈpændə/ a rare species of black and white animal which looks like a bear

paralysed (adj) *60* /ˈpærəlaɪzd/ unable to move

part (n) *19* /pɑːt/ *(in this context)* role or person you are going to be in a role-play

participants (n) *38* /pɑːˈtɪsɪpənts/ the people taking part in an activity

patient (n) *77* /ˈpeɪʃənt/ someone who is ill and is receiving help from a doctor

pen-friend (n) *13* /ˈpenfrend/ someone (usually from another country) you make friends with by letter

performance (n) *38* /pəˈfɔːməns/ how well or badly a sport or activity is done

physical (adj) *52* /ˈfɪzɪkəl/ related to the body

Physics (n) *12* /ˈfɪzɪks/ the science concerned with the study of objects and natural forces

pierced (adj) *6* /ˈpɪəst/ a hole made in your skin so you can wear an earring in it

planet (n) *58* /ˈplænɪt/ a large round object that moves around a star

playful (adj) *24* /ˈpleɪfəl/ wanting to play

point (v) *60* /pɔɪnt/ to show something (with your finger)

pole (n) *50* /pəʊl/ a stick or post

pollution (n) *83* /pəˈluːʃən/ contamination, the process of making something dirty or dangerous

poor (adj) *26* /pɔː/ not good

practise (v) *50* /ˈpræktɪs/ to use a particular method

precise (adj) *11* /prɪˈsaɪs/ exact

prediction (n) *52* /prɪˈdɪkʃən/ saying what is going to happen in the future

prepare (v) *59* /prɪˈpeə/ to make something ready

prevention (n) *22* /prɪˈvenʃən/ the act of stopping something from taking place

profession (n) *64* /prəˈfeʃən/ a job that needs special education or training

project (n) *33* /ˈprɒdʒekt/ a plan

pronounced (v) *19* /prəˈnaʊnst/ the way to say something

prospects (n) *10* /ˈprɒspekts/ opportunities, chances of future success

provider (n) *10* /prəˈvaɪdə/ someone who provides something e.g. money (especially for a family)

provincial (adj) *66* /prəˈvɪnʃəl/ parts of the country that are not near the capital city

pull out (pv) *50* /pʊl ˈaʊt/ to take out, extract

Q

quiet (adj) *24* /ˈkwɪət/ not making much noise

R

rare (adj) *32* /reə/ not seen or found very often

reaction (n) *28* /rɪˈækʃən/ *(in this context)* a bad effect

reason (n) *32* /ˈriːzən/ cause, explanation for something that has happened

recommend (v) *50* /rekəˈmend/ to advise someone to do something

recycle (v) *83* /riːˈsaɪkəl/ to use materials such as glass, paper again

reduce (v) *66* /rɪˈduːs/ to make less

refuse (v) *14* /rɪˈfjuːz/ to say 'no'

relate (to) (v) *38* /rɪˈleɪt/ *(in this context)* to have a connection with

relax (v) *34* /rɪˈlæks/ to be calm, peaceful, enjoy free time

remedy (n) *50* /ˈremədi/ a medicine to cure an illness or injury

reporter (n) *19* /rɪˈpɔːtə/ a person who writes reports for a newspaper or news programme

resolution (n) *55* /rezəˈluːʃən/ a promise to yourself to do something

respect (v) *48* /rɪˈspekt/ to admire someone because they have high standards

results (n) *12* /rɪˈzʌlts/ *(in this context)* how successful something is

role card (np) *19* /ˈrəʊl kaːd/ text which shows the person you are going to be in a role play activity

romance (n) *36* /rəʊˈmæns/ a film/book about love

rubbish (n) *83* /ˈrʌbɪʃ/ the things we throw away e.g. old newspapers, empty tins

rubbish (n)(infml) *10* /ˈrʌbɪʃ/ something that is bad, not correct

rude (adj) *36* /ruːd/ not very polite, slightly offensive

run away (pv) *46* /rʌn əˈweɪ/ to leave without telling anyone where you are going

run on (pv) *83* /ˈrʌn ɒn/ to be powered by, use

run out (pv) *83* /rʌn ˈaʊt/ to be finished, no longer available

rush (v) *12* /rʌʃ/ to be in a hurry

S

scared (adj) *66* /skeəd/ frightened or nervous about something

scary (adj)(infml) *24* /ˈskeərɪ/ frightening

science fiction (np) *36* /saɪəns ˈfɪkʃən/ a film or book about imaginary scientific developments in the future and their effects on life

scratch (v) *58* /skrætʃ/ to hurt your skin with something hard and sharp

sensitive (adj) *10* /ˈsensətɪv/ able to understand people's feelings, problems

shake (v) *34* /ʃeɪk/ to move up and down or from side to side quickly

share (v) *46* /ˈʃeə/ to tell someone about a problem

silly (adj) *19* /ˈsɪlɪ/ not sensible, reasonable or practical

sink (v) *34* /sɪnk/ to go down below the surface of water

slightly (adv) *77* /ˈslaɪtlɪ/ a little

slimy (adj) *24* /ˈslaɪmɪ/ something that appears to be wet

snack bar (n) *77* /ˈsnæk bɑː/ a place where you can buy sandwiches and other fast food

so far (adv) *39* /ˈsəʊ fɑː/ up until now

so-called (adj) *54* /səʊ ˈkɔːld/ an expression used to describe something that may be wrongly named

solar power (np) *83* /səʊlə ˈpaʊə/ electrical power generated by the sun

spare time (np) *14* /speə ˈtaɪm/ free time, time when you are not working

special (adj) *78* /ˈspeʃəl/ unusual, not ordinary

special effects (np) *36* /ˈspeʃəl ɪˈfekts/ an unusual image that has been produced artificially for a film

speed (n) *34* /spiːd/ how fast something travels

spoilt (adj) *67* /spɔɪlt/ someone who has everything they want and, as a result, behaves badly

spot (v) *34* /spɒt/ to see, notice something in the distance

staff (n) *64* /stɑːf/ workers in an organisation (singular = a member of staff)

star (n) *38* /stɑː/ a famous and successful performer in entertainment or sport

stare (v) *58* /steə/ to look at something for a long time without moving your eyes

statement (n) *14* /ˈsteɪtmənt/ something that is written, said or reported to let people know your opinion

statistics (n) *10* /stəˈtɪstɪks/ a collection of numbers which represent facts or measurements

steal (v) *87* /stiːl/ to take something which does not belong to you

stem sentences (np) *67* /stem ˈsentənsɪz/ the beginnings of sentences given in a language activity which the student completes

still (adv) *39* /stɪl/ continue to

still have (adv phr) *32* /ˈstɪl hæv/ continue to have

straight (adj) *57* /streɪt/ not curly

strange (adj) *50* /streɪndʒ/ unusual, surprising

stress-related (adj) *52* /stres rɪˈleɪtɪd/ connected with tension and anxiety

striped (adj) *50* /straɪpt/ having lines or bands of colour close together

stylish (adj) *18* /ˈstaɪlɪʃ/ attractive in a fashionable way

suitable (adj) *24* /ˈsuːtəbəl/ having the right qualities for a particular situation

supportive (adj) *46* /səˈpɔːtɪv/ giving someone help when they are having problems

T

tailor (n) *18* /ˈteɪlə/ someone who makes clothes, especially men's suits

take something (I'll take it) (vp) *16* /ˈteɪk sʌmθɪŋ/ *(in this context)* to buy, to have

taste (n) *8* /teɪst/ personal choice (of clothes, music)

taste (v) *26* /teɪst/ to put something in your mouth to see if it is good to eat

technical training (n) *18* /ˈteknɪkəl ˈtreɪnɪŋ/ a situation in which you learn practical skills

teenager (n) *6* /ˈtiːneɪdʒə/ a person between 13 and 19 years old

(that) counts (ce) *19* /kaʊnts/ *(in this context)* that is important

these days (np) *64* /ðiːz 'deɪz/ today, in modern times

thriller (n) *36* /θrɪlə/ a film (or book) that tells an exciting story about murder or crime

tie (n) *62* /taɪ/ a long piece of material men wear round their necks

tingle (v) *28* /tɪŋgl/ to feel a pricking sensation, an unpleasant feeling

tiny (adj) *58* /'taɪnɪ/ extremely small

topic (n) *59* /'tɒpɪk/ subject

tournament (n) *38* /'tɔːnəmənt/ a competition of a series of games played until there is one winner

traditional (adj) *50* /trə'dɪʃənəl/ *(in this context)* the way something has been for a long time

tragic (adj) *34* /trædʒɪk/ a sad event that involves death

trainers (n) *62* /'treɪnəz/ a type of strong shoe you wear for sport

translator (n) *58* /træns'leɪtə/ someone who changes speech or writing into another language

transport (n) *51* /'trænspɔːt/ a system of taking people or things from one place to another (e.g. train)

treatment (n) *50* /triːtmənt/ a method used to cure an illness or injury

trick (n) *36* /trɪk/ *(in this context)* a joke

tumour (n) *42* /'tjuːmə/ a mass of cells in your body that have increased in size too quickly

turn away (pv) *34* /tɜːn ə'weɪ/ to move in a different direction from someone or something

TV documentary (np) *32* /tiːviː dokjːu'mentrɪ/ a television programme giving facts about a subject

U

ugly (adj) *24* /ʌglɪ/ unattractive, unpleasant to look at

unfold (v) *34* *(in this context)* /ʌn'fəʊld/ to take place, to become clear

unique (adj) *30* /juː'niːk/ unlike anything else

V

valuables (n) *87* /'væljuəbəlz/ things which are precious, such as jewellery, passports, money

vegetarian (n) *29* /vedʒə'teərɪən/ a person who does not eat meat or fish

vet (veterinary surgeon) (n) *22* /vet/ an animal doctor

videophone (n) *83* /'vɪdɪəʊ fəʊn/ a phone with a TV screen so you can see who is calling

voyage (n) *79* /'vɔɪ-ɪdʒ/ a journey by sea

W

waistcoat (n) *20* /'weɪstkəʊt/ a piece of clothing without arms that you wear over a shirt

warn (v) *34* /wɔːn/ to tell someone that something bad or dangerous might happen

wavy (adj) *56* /'weɪvɪ/ not straight

weak (adj) *22* /wiːk/ not strong

what else? (adv phr) *15* /wɒt 'els/ what other things?

wicked (adj) *8* /'wɪkɪd/ great, fantastic, cool

wide range (np) *50* /waɪd 'reɪndʒ/ a variety of, a large number of

wild (in the) (n) *32* /waɪld/ in natural and free conditions

within reason (adv) *62* /wɪðɪn 'rɪːzən/ within sensible limits

worm (n) *24* /wɜːm/ a long thin creature with no legs that lives in soil

worry (about) (v) *21* /'wʌrɪ/ to be concerned or anxious (about) something

worrying (adj) *27* /'wʌriɪŋ/ something that causes concern

worse (adj) *51* /wɜːs/ when a thing or person is not as good as another in its group

Y

youngster (n) *66* /'jʌŋstə/ a young person (a word usually used by older people)

youth club (n) *8* /'juːð klʌb/ a supervised place where young people can meet

Z

zoo (zoological garden) (n) *32* /zuː/ a place where living, wild animals are kept

Table of irregular verbs

Infinitive	Simple past	Past participle
ban	banned	banned
be	was/were	been
become	became	become
break	broke	broken
bring	brought	brought
build	built	built
buy	bought	bought
choose	chose	chosen
cut	cut	cut
do	did	done
eat	ate	eaten
feel	felt	felt
fight	fought	fought
find	found	found
get	got	got
give	gave	given
go	went	gone
grow	grew	grown
hang	hung	hung
have	had	had
hit	hit	hit
learn	learnt	learnt
leave	left	left
lose	lost	lost
make	made	made
meet	met	met
pay	paid	paid
put	put	put
read	read	read
run	ran	run
see	saw	seen
shake	shook	shaken
sing	sang	sung
sink	sank	sunk
spend	spent	spent
spin	spun	spun
steal	stole	stolen
take	took	taken
tell	told	told
think	thought	thought
try	tried	tried
wear	wore	worn
win	won	won
write	wrote	written